You Don't Look Like a Librarian

You Don't Look Like a Librarian

Shattering Stereotypes and Creating Positive New Images in the Internet Age

Ruth Kneale

Information Today, Inc.
Medford, New Jersey

First Printing, 2009

You Don't Look Like a Librarian: Shattering Stereotypes and Creating Positive New Images in the Internet Age

Library of Congress Cataloging-in-Publication Data

Kneale, Ruth, 1968-
    You don't look like a librarian : shattering stereotypes and creating positive new images in the Internet age / Ruth Kneale.
        p. cm.
    Includes bibliographical references and index.
        ISBN 978-1-57387-366-6
1. Librarian--Public opinion. 2. Librarians--Attitudes. 3. Librarians--Effect of technological innovations on. 4. Librarians--Job descriptions. I. Title
    Z682.K645 2009
    020.92--dc22

                                                                    2009000421

Printed and bound in the United States of America.

President and CEO: Thomas H. Hogan, Sr.
Editor-in-Chief and Publisher: John B. Bryans
Managing Editor: Amy M. Reeve
VP Graphics and Production: M. Heide Dengler
Book Designer: Kara Mia Jalkowski
Cover Designer: Danielle Nicotra
Copyeditor: Dorothy Pike
Proofreader: Pat Hadley-Miller
Indexer: Sharon Hughes

www.infotoday.com

CONTENTS

Acknowledgments

To the librarians around the world who have emailed me examples—both positive and negative—of librarians in the media and in the workplace and given me such a rich trove of material to work with: Thank you all.

I want to extend a special thanks to the librarians who let me interview them for this book: Stephen Abram, Amy Buckland, Laura Carscaddon, Andrew Evans, Abigail Goben, Amy Hale-Janeke, Jill Hurst-Wahl, Jill Jarrell, Parker Ladwig, Jenny Levine, Joe Murphy, Joshua Neff, Kathleen Robertson, and Shannon Smith. I also want to thank Kathy Dempsey for her support through the years, John Bryans for never giving up on me, and Rachel Singer Gordon for her patience and fortitude. Without all of you, this book wouldn't have happened.

Last but absolutely not least, to my parents for all their support, and to Reagan and Isaac, my husband and son, who put up with all the drama and time away that went into creating this book. Dmuvh!

ABOUT THE WEBPAGE

www.librarian-image.net/book

As you may have noticed, dozens of newspaper articles, books, movies, music, toys, tees, calendars, ads, and other items talk about, hint at, reference, or otherwise nod to the image of librarians. Many online representations are mentioned in this book, but due to the ever-malleable nature of the web, sites may move or vanish, and new sites are appearing all the time.

The companion webpage for this book (www.librarian-image.net/book) contains a list of all the resources, references, and websites mentioned in this book, plus a few others that may be of interest. I'll regularly check the links for ongoing validity, and new items will be added as appropriate. Please continue to email suggestions and items of interest to ruth.kneale@gmail.com.

Disclaimer

Neither the publisher nor the author make any claim as to the results that may be obtained through the use of this webpage or of any of the Internet resources it references or links to. Neither publisher nor author will be held liable for any results, or lack thereof, obtained by the use of this page or any of its links; for any third-party charges; or for any hardware, software, or other problems that may occur as the result of using it. This webpage is subject to change or discontinuation without notice at the discretion of the publisher and author.

FOREWORD

I have a confession to make.

Whenever I'm outside the convention center at library conferences, I play "Guess the Librarian." The woman with the sneakers? The man with the bow-tie? Definitely not the person with the briefcase! (For those who want to play along at home, it doesn't count as a guess if the person is holding a bag from a library vendor or publisher.)

It's all about being able to figure out not only *who* is a librarian, but also what type of librarian they are. The guybrarian? The cool gamer? The stuffy academic? The fabulous administrator?

If there is one thing all librarians share, it's the response we get when we go to library school: "You need a masters degree to learn how to say 'shhh?!' Here's the chain to hold your eyeglasses!" Perhaps we are so sensitive to librarian representations in pop culture *because* of how well we know these stereotypes.

In *You Don't Look Like a Librarian*, Ruth Kneale addresses the image of librarians—in libraryland and out in the greater world—using both fictional/pop culture references and real-life experiences to show that librarians are more than the sum of their stereotypes.

This book is entertaining and light-hearted but also quite serious. Sure, it's fun to talk about what librarians look or don't look like, but take that a step further. Connect the dots from the assumptions people make about librarians to how the public perceives us, and you'll quickly realize the impact stereotypes have on everything from customer expectations to salaries.

When community members don't come in to use the library because of an image they have in their head of what libraries and librarians are (and aren't), we lose customers.

When officials and taxpayers vote down library budgets or ask to decrease them because they aren't aware of all that the library offers, we have a problem.

But this is not the community's problem: It's *our* problem, the problem of not marketing who we are and what we do.

This isn't about tossing out your sensible shoes and cardigans; I proudly wear both. But it is about letting people know: We don't go 'shhh.' We're not hiding in dusty carrels, more comfortable with books than people. We *do* know technology, whether we're helping someone to find a job site or to download photos of their grandchildren. Yes, we have a print edition of Jane Austen's *Pride and Prejudice*, but we also have the DVD of Gurinder Chadha's *Bride & Prejudice*.

This book has a lot to offer. You'll be nodding your head in recognition—and looking for the many books, movies, and comics it references. It will introduce you to peers who are challenging stereotypes through the work they do. Most importantly, it will make you think about what it really means to be a librarian. *You Don't Look Like a Librarian* will help you brainstorm ways to market yourself, and your library, so that your community will recognize that today's library is more than just a warm building with great books: It's also the heart of the community.

One of these days, as Ruth Kneale makes very clear, it's going to be impossible to play—and win—"Guess the Librarian!"

—Elizabeth Burns

Elizabeth Burns is currently a Youth Services Consultant for a regional library for the National Library Service for the Blind and Physically Handicapped. She writes about books, movies, and television at A Chair, A Fireplace, & A Tea Cozy (yzocaet.blogspot.com) and about pop culture and libraries at Pop Goes the Library (www.popgoesthelibrary.com). Along with Sophie Brookover, she is the author of *Pop Goes the Library: Using Pop Culture to Connect With Your Whole Community.*

INTRODUCTION

As a general rule, librarians are a kick in the pants socially, often full of good humor, progressive, and, naturally, well read. They tend to be generalists who know so much about so many things that they are quite the opposite of the boring old poops they have been made out to be. Most of them are full of life, some even full of the devil.

—Bill Hall, editorial page editor, *Lewiston (Idaho) Tribune*, September 19, 2001

My name is Ruth, and I am a librarian!

In my imagination, at this point, you're saying "OK … great quote, but so? What's so special about this book, and why should I buy it?" So let me start by introducing myself and my mission—and hopefully I'll convince you!

My first years in library work were not actually spent as a librarian, as defined by Dictionary.com's various sources as "a professional person trained in library science and engaged in library services." I started as a "document coordinator," in charge of all the documentation for an engineering construction project. I'd always spent my time in libraries, though: My mother was a career librarian, so I tended to be in and around (and sometimes under) them my entire life. I also have some obsessive tendencies (which I freely admit!), and the idea of pairing my organizational interests with these tendencies really sparked a fire of interest in the organization of information. Maybe I wouldn't work in the kind of library I grew up in, but I'd work in some type of library, nonetheless. At this point in the mid-1990s, I was also pondering going back to school for an advanced degree. Accordingly, I wandered down the street to the University of Arizona's School of Information Resources and Library Science to meet with an advisor. (Hi, Dr. Seavey!) As it turns out, there are a lot of librarians that do what I do—they're classified as special librarians—and the school was just starting to change its focus to include more "technical" fields as well as the traditional ones. I was hooked!

Not two weeks after I started graduate school in 1997, I heard my very first cheerful comment from a co-worker who overheard me discussing my class schedule with our boss: "But you can't be a librarian—you don't look like one!" I heard this, or the more common "but you don't look like a librarian!" variation, so often during grad school—on trips, in casual conversation, all over the place—that I decided to change my email signature file until I didn't hear it again. It read: "But you don't look like a librarian! Yeah, I get that a lot." I thought these comments came just because I was young, had a somewhat experimental hairstyle, and had many, many earrings, and expected that in a month or two I would change my signature file. Well, I was still using that quote two years later, after I graduated from library school and went on to my first post-school job in Hawaii.

A year later, following a series of similar comments, I realized the situation was much larger and much more complicated than I'd originally suspected. I set out on a mission to examine why folks kept saying that, to see what they thought a librarian was supposed to look like, and to explain that we come in all shapes, sizes, and colors. I created the original "Do you look like a librarian?" survey (see Appendix A), which became the first step on the path to this book. Since then, I have learned that we as a profession tend to be just a bit hyperaware of how folks perceive us. As Grant Burns says in his critical bibliography on librarians in fiction, "An examination of relevant works shows that librarians have been somewhat preoccupied with their image nearly since the inception of the profession." (His own book being yet another navel-gazing entry in that genre!) Since my initial realization in 2000 that this issue was bigger than I'd realized, I've conducted three surveys, given three major presentations, spoken many times to groups of librarians and nonlibrarians, and written several articles on the topic. Here we are in 2009, long after I thought librarians' image would no longer be of any interest, yet the issue is still with us—and very much alive!

Why, in this increasingly digital age, do so many people still think of librarians as bespectacled, shushing grumps? At the end of the 1990s, we were facing an information explosion. Other professions formerly considered "geeky" or "nerdy" (computer programmers, database administrators—not to mention a nifty new profession in the picture: webmaster) were starting to be seen as cool and groovy. But, what happened to us librarians? Before the Net broke loose on the world, librarians provided access to giant amounts of information. We deal with computers every day, we administer databases, we are masters of our library websites. Who better to help guide people along than us, those trained to surf the flood? But no: Not only did I not look like a librarian, librarians couldn't help—and weren't wanted—in the digital age, because "everything's going on the Internet and I can find it myself!"

Phooey to that! We now begin to see the untruth in that naive statement. Yet, there are still people—lots and lots of people—who don't see librarians as informed and useful professionals who are skilled in information knowledge and organization.

How can we change this perception? What can we do? And what are some of the images being presented to the Great American Public these days that bump headfirst into our reality? This book will cover the stereotype, media images of librarians, how 21st-century librarians are breaking stereotypes with their everyday work, and some thoughts on the future.

I hope you'll take a read. Cheers!

STEREOTYPES? WHAT STEREOTYPES?

In the public psyche, a librarian is a woman of indeterminate age, who wears spectacles; a person with either a timorous disposition or an austere disposition, wearing a long sleeved blouse buttoned to the neck; someone who loves silence, likes books, and suffers people. Librarians don't laugh. They are covered with a thin film of dust. They have pale skins, which, when touched (as if one ever could) might flake and prove to be reptilian scales.

—Barry Bowes, *Between the Stacks* (1979)

Even if you aren't working in the field, chances are that you've run across the commonly held stereotype of librarians. Ask any Joe or Jane Q. Public what comes to mind when they think of a librarian. They'll inevitably describe an older woman, her hair in a tight bun, wearing glasses, a cardigan, and sensible (meaning ugly) shoes, who wouldn't know a computer from a cat (of which she owns many). She usually says "Shh" a lot, too!

As for those of us who don't quite match this image, the usual response is along the lines of: "But you don't look like a librarian!"

What, exactly, are we supposed to look like? This is an interesting question, and feeds into many societal expectations: gender, age, sexuality, type of work, level of work, professionalism, education, social ability, and so much more. But, you may wonder, "So what? Why should it matter to me what someone thinks a librarian should look like?" Well, I'll tell you why. It matters:

- When a patron doesn't ask you for help on the computer because "you're a girl."

- When someone approaches a library help desk but waits for a woman to arrive because "everyone knows that men can't be librarians."

- When two people who do the same tasks are paid differently if one of them has "librarian" in their job title (and you know which one is paid less).

- When librarians are reclassified at a lower pay rate, as happened in February 2008 at the Marathon County (WI) Public Library (www.lisnews.org/node/29261), because their board thinks librarians today "do less complex work."

- When "the services and functions that librarians provide in their day-to-day work and the value they play to those they serve are often overlooked,

by both those inside and outside the profession"
(*The Image and Role of the Librarian*).

• When recent computer games continue to show
interactive librarian characters as cranky, shushing,
old ladies. The librarian character in the September
2007 game MySims for the Wii, for instance, is an
older lady with bunned hair and glasses; her idling
animations are reading, stamping books, shuffling
paper, and telling people to be quiet.

• When patrons lose out on knowledge and learning
because they assume we can't help them. As Linda
Absher notes, "in the mind of the patron, the
stereotype of the librarian as gate-keeper impedes
access to services."

It's all about the marketing ... marketing, marketing,
marketing! The *Encyclopaedia Britannica* defines marketing as "the sum of activities involved in directing the flow
of goods and services from producers to consumers"
(www.britannica.com/EBchecked/topic/365730/
marketing). Speaking at the 2008 SLA Annual Meeting,
marketing guru Seth Godin tells us to "Be remarkable"
and that "Ideas that spread win, and librarians know how
to spread ideas." We need to get busy spreading the great
ideas about our remarkableness, our profession, and our
capabilities. On a one-to-one basis, things may not seem
that bad. Librarians tell me about receiving effusive
thanks from a patron for helping them—generally, a
patron who hadn't realized before what librarians could

do. This makes me wonder, though, how many patrons are being shortchanged just because they *don't* know all the things we can do.

In the bigger picture, we're still lacking. How we are perceived and thought of *directly* affects how our patron groups, whatever they may be, approach us and use our skills. How we are represented has a direct impact on our day-to-day existence. How do we look? How do we sound? What are we wearing? What do we do when we're not shelving books? Whether we like it or not, whether we agree or not, all of these things and more affect what our patrons think of us—which directly impacts how our patrons interact with us. According to Maura Seale, "User perceptions negatively affect the ability of librarians to meet information needs, simply because a profession cannot serve those who do not understand its purpose and expertise."

Another issue involves our various job titles, most of which aren't very descriptive of librarians' actual duties. (Then again, I suppose you could say that about almost any job out there these days.) Marvel at the giant list of job titles being used today by librarians by visiting and contributing to Michelle Mach's "Real Job Titles for Librarians and Information Science Professionals" (www.michellemach.com/jobtitles/realjobs.html). The librarians I interviewed for this book (you'll meet them in Chapter 3) go by titles as varied as:

- Assistant librarian

- Digital services librarian

- Government documents librarian

- Head of reference

- Information consultant

- Information resource specialist

- Librarian

- Mathematics and life sciences librarian

- President

- Teen services librarian

- Vice president

- Youth services librarian

As I've discovered over the course of many surveys and conversations throughout the years, this is just the tip of the title iceberg; find more discussion of job titles in Appendix A.

Librarians are called anything and everything these days. But, what does this really mean? I worked long and hard for my advanced degree in librarianship, so was disturbed and depressed after graduation to realize I could make a lot more money doing exactly the same work in the corporate world—in a job that didn't have "librarian" in its title. Perception directly influences salaries and promotion opportunities in the workplace. According to the U.S. Bureau of Labor Statistics (BLS; www.bls.gov), the

2000 median salary for librarians in the U.S. was $42,730. The 2000 occupation definition (stats.bls.gov/oes/2000/oes254021.htm) states that librarians: "Administer libraries and perform related library services. Work in a variety of settings, including public libraries, schools, colleges and universities, museums, corporations, government agencies, law firms, non-profit organizations, and healthcare providers. Tasks may include selecting, acquiring, cataloguing, classifying, circulating, and maintaining library materials; and furnishing reference, bibliographical, and readers' advisory services. May perform in-depth, strategic research, and synthesize, analyze, edit, and filter information. May set up or work with databases and information systems to catalogue and access information."

This nicely summarizes a huge number of responsibilities. Let's pay attention to that last line, though. "May set up or work with databases and information systems to catalogue and access information" is also often a job requirement for database administrators. Looking at the median salary for database administrators in 2000 (stats.bls.gov/oes/2000/oes151061.htm), at $51,990, it's 21.5 percent higher than that of librarians. On the (slightly) up side, the same data for 2007 (www.bls.gov/oes/current/oes254021.htm) shows that librarians' median salary rose to $50,970—but the median 2007 salary for database administrators has risen to $67,250 (www.bls.gov/oes/current/oes151061.htm), which is 32 percent higher than that of librarians. Librarians often also serve as webmasters, web designers, or web developers for their organizations, which the BLS lumps into the category "Computer Scientists and Database Administrators" (www.bls.gov/oco/ocos042.htm). The 2007 median salary for web administrators is listed as $62,250; for web developers, $68,125; and for web designers, $59,250—all quite comfortably above librarians' median salaries. The discrepancy seems to be growing larger, rather than smaller, as time progresses.

Yes, but that's the government. What about in the real world? Let's take a look at some current job advertisements. Now, as we all know, librarians have about a zillion different job titles. To keep things evenly measurable, we'll look for jobs using the same keywords as used by the BLS. As of this writing, the huge job clearance site Monster (www.monster.com) listed:

- 156 jobs for librarians: Monster's stated median expected salary for "a typical librarian in the United States" is $55,018 (tinyurl.com/6bcylr). (Higher than the BLS numbers.)

- 2,607 listings for database administrators: Monster's median expected salary for a typical database administrator in the U.S. is $83,706 (tinyurl.com/6j7x77).

- 157 jobs for webmasters: Monster.com's median expected salary for a typical webmaster in the U.S. is $64,049 (tinyurl.com/6e9n6k).

Even in the "real world" of competitive employment, salaries vary substantially based on job title. You can rearrange job duties; you can stuff a lot into "performs a variety of tasks" and "other duties as required," but the job title, in most cases, determines salary.

This leads to another problem, as well. Compare tech-savvy librarians' skills to their salaries, and some are concerned about a "brain drain" of librarians into the corporate world, where they can do the same tasks at a higher salary—and without the "L word" in their title. This is a tough decision for many of us: Are we in the profession for the money, or are we in it for the satisfaction of the work? Another perceived appeal of the corporate world over libraries is simply technological excitement. We've all heard of, or experienced, library workplaces with restrictive policies on installing new software or interacting online (disallowing instant messaging or Firefox, anyone?), and we've all seen environments that fail to encourage innovation. As Jonathan Rochkind puts it in one entry on his Bibliographic Wilderness blog (bibwild.wordpress.com/2008/02/04/brain-drain), "If libraries can't hold on to smart future-oriented people who understand the role technology can play in creating an exciting future for us—the prospects of libraries accepting the mantle of innovation also seem dim." Thankfully, we're seeing more and more libraries opening their arms (and their IT restrictions) to tech-savvy librarians, encouraging them to help create that future and helping keep our best and brightest in the library world. You'll read about some of these librarians in Chapter 3 and about forward-thinking libraries seeing increases in usage and positive press. Many of us also thrive on challenge—and the challenge of bringing our libraries forward into the networked world is very enticing. I can report that there are a lot of folks itching to stay in librarianship and advance that techno-excitement!

Popular Perceptions

We've seen a lot of discussion over the past 10 years or so about appearance, impressions, and image. As noted in so many places, we are a navel-gazing profession. We see these topics come up repeatedly in articles and columns in professional publications, but much more so these days in participatory discussions on blogs and wikis. Some seminal resources include:

- Antony Brewerton's 1999 article, "Wear Lipstick, Have a Tattoo, Belly-dance, Then Get Naked: The Making of a Virtual Librarian," in *Impact: The Journal of the Career Development Group* (tinyurl.com/6lffhk), pulled together a comprehensive collection of the online resources available at the time. Some are still around and are still having an impact on us. He comments that "friends—and strangers—are always willing to give me fresh examples of (usually quite appalling) representations of libraries and library workers in the popular media." (I find myself in the same situation these days!) His article was also the featured headliner in Volume 1, Number 1, of *NewBreed Librarian* (scholarsbank.uoregon. edu/dspace/handle/1794/1071), a webzine active from 2001 to 2002 (sadly, now defunct; it was a great resource for new librarians).

- In 2001, Heather Acerro, Adrienne Allen, Cheryl Bartel, DarLynn Nemitz, and Dana Vinke put together a great website investigating the "Image of Libraries in Popular Culture" (besser.tsoa.nyu.edu/impact/f01/Focus/Image/index.htm). Their site looks into "what these images signify about our profession and about the culture which produces them."

- Volume 78 of *The Reference Librarian*, consisting of 10 articles on the topic, was collected and co-released as the scholarly publication *The Image and Role of the Librarian* in 2002. As editors Wendi Arant and Candace Benefiel say in the preface, "There seems to be no profession as preoccupied with self-examination as that of librarianship. While some of it may stem from an identity crisis, the refrain heard over and over is startlingly similar to Rodney Dangerfield's 'I don't get no respect.' This seems to be true of all types of librarians— from public librarians who (often rightly) complain of being treated like servants by the patrons they serve, to the academic librarians who are always trying to establish their 'faculty-ness' to the teaching professors." We'll see that the passage of a few years has had little effect; modern librarians share recent stories (in Chapter 3) that strikingly parallel the examples Arant and Benefiel used when they wrote their preface.

- A short-lived blog "SSSSHHHHHH!!!!!" (stereotypicallibrarian.blogspot.com) from 2006 collected stories and photos from librarians and library workers related to the stereotype—and showed how they emphatically did *not* fit that stereotype.

- In 2007, Kathleen Low published *Casanova Was a Librarian*, a "light-hearted look at the profession."

- In the spring of 2008, the Oregon Library Association's *OLA Quarterly* newsletter focused on "Lively Librarians Loose in the Limelight: Libraries in Popular Media"; many other professional library publications have also recently published articles on the topic. (In other words—not even counting the blogs—our preoccupation with stereotypes is pervasive.)

- A regular column in *Library Journal* called "NextGen" (go to www.libraryjournal.com and search for "NextGen") often discusses issues related to image and the profession.

- The Popular Culture Association has a section called Libraries, Archives, Museums, and Popular Culture Area that regularly discusses librarians in popular culture (www.pcaaca.org/areas/libraries.php).

Interestingly—and vaguely creepily—there's an entire sub-stereotype related to sexuality. One perception of librarians is that of a sexually repressed middle-aged (or younger) woman, just waiting for the right guy to come along so she can take off her glasses, let down her hair, and release the wild sex-crazy animal within. *Playboy* especially seems to use the "sexy librarian" concept a lot, and an entire pornographic subculture (both books and movies) is devoted to librarians (and yes, there's a website that catalogs them all!). It turns out that several dominatrices advertise being a librarian among their specialties ("She likes a little disorder with her Dewey."). Jessamyn West, librarian and biblioblogger extraordinaire, hosts a collection of bookplates and images of naked librarians at her site ... and there are a lot of them. (Find links to both the librarians in porn site and Jessamyn's collection at www.libraryunderground.org/sexuality.htm; be aware that this link contains adult content.)

On the other side of things, if you're a male librarian, no matter your age, people assume you must be gay. I can't tell you the number of emails I've gotten from guy librarians (not guybrarians, thank you very much) over the years who've told me that this is their only experience with the stereotypical image.

We're More Than Our Stereotype

I've talked to a lot of librarians over the years. Just about every one of them has a story to share about confounding people's perceptions, whether their tale is about the time a patron was amazed when the librarian found an answer to his question using a computer database, or about how at a casual gathering she heard the inevitable comment "But librarians can't do X" tossed around. Here are just a few of their stories:

- From a school librarian: "I once had a 7th grade student library aide who was definitely not the sharpest knife in the drawer. I almost always had to undo the work that she had done, but she obviously loved 'helping,' so I used to save the easiest tasks for her to do. Open House night arrived, and her mother dropped in to talk to me. She gushed on and on about how much her daughter enjoyed being a library aide, and crowned it all by saying, 'You know, my daughter is not very bright, so I figure when she grows up, maybe she can be a librarian.' I SWEAR this is true—a word-for-word quote. I was speechless!"

- From a public librarian: "I was closing down a bank account in one town because I was moving to another town where I was just hired to work at the public library. The teller asked me what my occupation was, and I told him librarian. He offered the title 'media specialist,' saying that sounded much better than librarian, because of all those things you (are supposed to) think of when you think of the term 'librarian.' I am sure I did not provoke him to this. All I wanted was to close my bank account, not hear some discourse on the stigmas associated with being a librarian. One thing about the incident that I thought was weird was that he never even bothered to 'catch himself' in the process of his insult. He just carried on and thought that his assessment of the profession was the norm."

- From a technology librarian: "I helped a friend who is a small business owner find some marketing information and she said 'I had no idea librarians knew how to do this stuff!'"

- From an academic librarian: "The most difficult one for me was perhaps the gentleman who was there with his son (who was probably in middle school—between 10 and 13 [years old], perhaps). He asked me if I could type up his son's paper while his son found pictures to use in the report because I didn't have anything to do other than read all the time. Luckily, I happened to have a stack of work to do at the desk that evening— while I would have loved to explain to him in a much stronger manner that I wasn't a secretary, I couldn't, because he was very sincere. I ended up explaining that I had a lot of work to do, and no, I couldn't type up his son's paper."

- Even the law librarians can't get away from the stereotype: "When I was working in another law firm, the associates decided that they wanted me to look like a librarian. So, they bought me a hair clip and horn-rimmed glasses and asked me to wear a long dress with a high collar so they could see me once as a librarian!"

I've also received a number of stories about the business-card game (mix up a bunch of business cards including yours and see if someone new, perhaps on an airplane, can pick yours out of the bunch; they never do because ... yeah, you know) and the bartender guessing game (gather a bunch of librarians to go to a bar—from a conference, meeting, whatever—and try to get the bartender to guess what they do; once again, nope, the poor bartender never guesses they're librarians).

In reality, librarians are so much more than the stereotype, in so many ways. Times have changed dramatically since the era of Marian the Librarian (*The Music Man* was released in 1962), and yet, even now, that outdated image persists. Why is that? Why do we see almost identical representations of librarians today? Why can't we shake Marian?

You may be shaking your head and thinking, "Yeah, but that isn't really the case now, is it? Those are outmoded, out-of-date ideas. Today's public sees the modern librarian for who he or she is." Well, think again. Following are some of the quotes posted in the early months of 2008 to just *two* of the worldwide Facebook sites about librarians: "No, I Don't Look Like a Librarian!" (www.facebook.com/group.php?gid=2251972614), which has 2,070 members at this writing, and "Yes, I Do Look Like a Librarian!" (www.facebook.com/group.php?gid=2272645001), which has 436 members and is growing:

- "I knew I was destined to be a librarian when I realized that I already dressed like one. Still, people usually say to me: 'You don't look like a librarian.' I reply: 'Yes I do; this is what a librarian looks like.'"

- From a librarian in Ireland: "Usually, I get 'Librarian? Sure, you're only a child!' I assure you I am not a child ..."

- "Because I'm a guy, I always get the WT*???? look."

- "It's hard for people to grasp that a 21st century librarian is not necessarily curled up in a corner, nose in book."

- "I work in a high school library and had a parent ask me if they could speak to an adult."

- From a male librarian in Australia: "Lady walks in, looks at me and suddenly points dramatically: 'You're not a woman!' 'Um, I guess not ...' Lady then turns her attention to the other guy on desk, gesturing wildly: 'You're not a woman either!' 'Not really, thanks for noticing!' Lady continues to stand there with a bewildered expression. We smile politely, nonplussed."

- From a London-based librarian: "So pleased to have found this group. Over the years, I've awarded myself a point each time someone says to me, 'Okay cut the bull***t, what do you really do for a living?' or similar when I tell them I'm a librarian. So far I've earned enough points to buy a Bentley Continental convertible or a holiday home in Nassau."

This is just one small sampling of librarians posting anecdotes and stories about the reactions they get when they reveal their profession; visit librarians' blogs or one of the other popular social networking sites to find similar stories. Here are some responses from my 2008 survey of librarians (read Appendix A for more):

- "I was sitting at the reference desk, just having come in from lunch, with my elbow-length curls flowing free and my John Lennon sunglasses still on, when two 50-something ladies came to the Circulation Desk and asked if we had a certain book. The student clerk pointed in my direction and said, 'You'll have to check LaserCat' (our CD-based OPAC). So the ladies came over and very gingerly asked, 'Excuse me sir—are you LaserCat?'"

- "My cell ringtone is a recognizable guitar part of a Guns & Roses song. I was offsite giving a training session to a group of high-level executives, and my cell rang. Embarrassed, I grabbed it and ran out of the room (thinking it was an emergency while I was away from home). When I walked back in and apologized, I was about to resume the session and noticed they were all smirking (all male meeting; I am a 'younger' female). The head of the meeting said 'I knew you weren't like the other librarians.'"

- "Folks expect me to be clueless and are shocked when I rock their worlds!"

Not a week goes by that I don't get an email, a Twitter, or a comment on my blog about yet another instance of "But you don't look like a librarian!" On the upside, we're starting to see some better portrayals, better representations, and a better understanding by Joe Q. Public about what it is librarians do. It's slow going, and for every positive portrayal in a book there are three unflattering portrayals in ads and movies, but at least we're moving forward. I would love to live and work in a world where anyone and everyone can be accepted as a librarian for their amazing skills, regardless of how they look or what they do for fun. But what else can we, as a profession, do to educate Joe and Jane Q. Public, and what are some of the varied ways we're portrayed in popular culture? Read on!

POP CULTURE
AND LIBRARIANS

It has long been supposed that the librarian is a quiet and docile member of society whose function is to do little more than reshelve books. Librarians are often depicted as old maids, as if the library were a repository for unmarried women. This, of course, is exactly what they want you to think.

—James Turner, Ordo Bibliotheca

Pop culture and librarians—ahh, what a great topic. Confronting and discussing the images of librarians as portrayed in the media always elicits some of the biggest gasps, and some of the biggest laughs. These images are fun to investigate, watch, read, or listen to—but they are still sometimes frustrating and seriously annoying. In this chapter, I'll explore how popular culture and the media have represented librarians. Everyone is familiar with the traditional stereotypes: Think Marian the Librarian from the musical *The Music Man*, or think about *It's a Wonderful Life*, where, without George in her life, poor

Mary is condemned to be the sad, spinsterish town librarian. But what about in this magical marvelous age of the Internet? Since we've exploded into an era of the worldwide sharing of knowledge, and since librarians have been the caretakers of that knowledge, has the presentation of librarians across various media changed along with the times? If so, what changes have we seen?

In the spring of 2008, Maura Seale published an interesting, if somewhat staid, article titled "Old Maids, Policemen, and Social Rejects: Mass Media Representations and Public Perceptions of Librarians" in the *Electronic Journal of Academic and Special Librarianship*. Similar to, but much shorter than, the 2002 collection *The Image and Role of the Librarian*, this article briefly investigated and discussed media representations of librarians. Seale identified five separate (but not discrete) categories of librarians as presented by mass media:

- The Old Maid, the most common category in pop culture, best described as our stereotypical image: a frumpy, prim, sexless, cranky old woman

- The Policeman, or the authoritative or fearsome librarian who holds power and control over library-goers

- The Parody, usually a comedic or satirical representation

- The Inept, meaning the socially inept or incompe-
  tent librarian who prefers the world of books to the
  real world

- The Hero/ine, positive portrayals of librarians in
  one way or another

In reviewing the books, movies, television shows, and
comics I've chosen as examples (all media representations
since 1990, and all chosen before Seale's essay was published), I find I am in surprising agreement with most of
her categorizations. It's surprising how easy it is to fit the
librarians described in the following sections into one of
these categories—some, in more than one. (Miss Zukas,
for example, fits into both the Old Maid and Policeman
categories, while Rupert Giles is both Inept and the
Hero.) Let's see if you agree.

Books

Countless books feature a librarian as a secondary or ter-
tiary character; this chapter would read like a phone book
if I addressed them all! If you have the interest and the
inclination to delve further, spend some time with Grant
Burns's thorough 1998 *Librarians in Fiction* bibliography
or check your local public library for reader's advisory
lists. Here, I'll discuss a few representative titles published within the last decade in which the librarian is the
main character. (Look for them in libraries everywhere!)

Here's a little popular fiction factoid: Did you know the author of *The Spiderwick Chronicles* is a librarian?

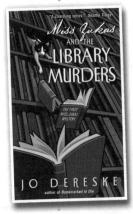

The Miss Zukas Series, by Jo Dereske

Please allow me to introduce you to Miss Wilhelmina Zukas, whom you may call Helma, but never Helm. The exceedingly particular and precise Miss Zukas is the librarian responsible for nonfiction history and applied sciences at the Bellehaven Public Library in Washington State. The first time we meet Helma, she is uncharacteristically late for work. (She leaves her blinds up, and the sun unexpectedly comes out; there's no help for it but that she must return home to lower the shades.) She arrives to find a dead body in the MO-NE aisle of the fiction stacks, and from that point on we're drawn into her world. A psychological profiler would probably classify Helma with obsessive-compulsive personality disorder; I think she just has fabulous attention to detail! This detail-oriented mind-set helps Helma (and her best friend Ruth, a Bohemian, Amazonian artist she's known since childhood) solve not just the first incidence of death in the library, but 10 more mysteries of mischief and mayhem. Along the way, we hear Helma's extreme expressions of "Oh, Faulkner!" when things get particularly sticky; get glimpses into Helma's Lithuanian heritage; witness her unwilling (yet somehow inevitable) opening up to a stray cat, stubbornly unnamed Boy Cat Zukas; and watch as Helma and Chief of Police Wayne Gallant tentatively dance closer and closer to an actual relationship.

The books in this series are (in order):

- *Miss Zukas and the Library Murders* (1994), where we first meet our cast of characters, and Helma helps answer the question of the body in the stacks.

- *Miss Zukas and the Island Murders* (1995), where Helma organizes her 20th high school reunion on a fog-shrouded island, and things go horribly awry.

- *Miss Zukas and the Stroke of Death* (1995), where we learn of Helma's canoeing skills and about the Snow to Surf Race, and Ruth is charged with murder.

- *Miss Zukas and the Raven's Dance* (1996), where Helma tackles curating a collection of Native American artifacts as well as the dead previous curator.

- *Out of Circulation* (1997), where Helma goes hiking in the Cascades, and a turn as a good Samaritan goes the wrong way.

- *Final Notice* (1998), where Helma's Aunt Em arrives from Michigan and brings her mysterious past with her.

- *Miss Zukas in Death's Shadow* (1999), where Helma becomes a murder suspect while performing community service at a homeless shelter.

- *Miss Zukas Shelves the Evidence* (2001), where Helma must solve an attack on Chief Gallant after meeting his teenage children for the first time.

- *Bookmarked to Die* (2006), where Helma deals with a batch of local authors, is made to attend group counseling sessions where the counselees keep showing up dead, and faces the disappearance of Boy Cat Zukas, all while celebrating her birthday.

- *Catalogue of Death* (2007), where Helma faces the loss of funding for the new library when the local benefactor is blown up on the construction site.

- *Index to Murder* (2008), the latest mystery, where Helma's organization and Ruth's artistic mayhem intersect over some stolen paintings.

All in all, I find this series highly enjoyable, although Helma may rub some librarians the wrong way. Yet, while she does personify some aspects of the stereotype, such as the ruthlessly tidy hair, respectable attire, and no-nonsense attitude, those characteristics could just as well be attributed to her obsessive-compulsive and somewhat antisocial behaviors. Her library co-workers definitely run the gamut of personalities, just as in a real library. The author, Jo Dereske, is herself a former librarian—and you can tell; it shines through in all the little details of life in the Bellehaven Public Library. While these stories may appear at first glance to fall within the stereotypical pattern, they also help highlight behind-the-scenes information about libraries and librarians. Most depictions of work in a library show librarians out in the public areas, either in the stacks or at the reference or circulation desks, but more often than not the action at the Bellehaven Public Library is conducted in the staff areas. Since part of the perception problem stems from the fact that people don't have a very good idea of what librarians do, reading about librarians' various responsibilities and the areas of action behind the scenes helps illuminate the hidden complexities of libraries. Additionally, Helma is definitely neither meek nor timid, other characteristics often assigned to the stereotype.

The Librarian,
by Larry Beinhart

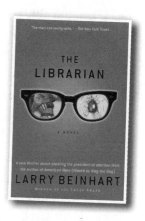

Murder! Conspiracy! Mayhem! Politics! Romance! Horses! Lies, deceit, and the Electoral College! Roll it all up, drop in a "nebbish" university librarian, and sit back: You're in for quite a ride. I personally found it quite difficult to put *The Librarian* down once I picked it up. (One word of warning, however: Folks of a politically conservative bent might find it a wee bit less thrilling.)

David Goldberg is a quiet, unassuming librarian who decides to pick up a bit of extra cash by moonlighting. So, he accepts a job cataloging the personal papers of an eccentric billionaire (to help a friend in need); said billionaire happens to be the driving impetus and funding source behind a secret society to steal the U.S. Presidency. To quote from the book jacket, "It's one of those moments when knowledge is a dangerous thing, and a little knowledge is even more dangerous, and the men with the guns want to kill the fellow indexing the archives."

In pursuit of his own safety (at first) then larger goals (later), David meets Niobe, who may not be what she seems. He discovers hidden depths in himself and his fellow librarians Susie and Inga, whom he drags into the chaos as well. Along the way, he ends up being charged with bestiality (nothing like a bit of extra shock value to stir the pot a bit) and pursued by the State of Virginia as a danger to self and others. Let's not forget he's also being hunted by the Department of Homeland Security, not to mention the security division of the aforementioned secret society. The book's resolution is, in itself, not a resolution at all; it is perhaps better described as an end to one set of questions and the beginning of another set. (It's hard to share information without giving anything away; there's a lot going on here!)

The portrayal of the librarians in this book is very believable and utterly practical. They are knowledgeable, interesting, resourceful, sexy, creative, and very good under pressure. Not a stereotype in sight! If all librarians were described and identified the way Beinhart portrays David, Susie, and Inga, I'd have a lot more free time on my hands!

The Jordan Poteet Series, by Jeff Abbott

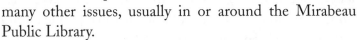

In this short series by author Jeff Abbott, we meet Jordan (Jordy) Poteet, recently returned to his hometown of Mirabeau, Texas, and working as the head librarian at the town's public library. The stories involve Jordy and the rest of the library staff dealing with censorship, freedom of information, real estate manipulation, environmentalism, and many other issues, usually in or around the Mirabeau Public Library.

Books in the series are (in order):

- *Do Unto Others* (2004), where Jordy butts heads with the town's religious fanatic over censorship. When he finds her dead body in the library a day after a very public disagreement, things look very grim indeed.

- *The Only Good Yankee* (2005), where a spate of mailbox explosions (including Jordy's girlfriend Candace's) rocks the town, and riverfront development is on everyone's mind.

- *Promises of Home* (2006), where Jordy and his childhood friends are forced to face a gruesome crime from the past.

- *Distant Blood* (2006), where Jordy meets his newly discovered family—only someone doesn't want to welcome him with open arms. (This book is the most powerful of the series, but also has the least to do with libraries or librarians, as it all takes place away from Mirabeau.)

Here, the lead character works as a librarian, and a lot of the action takes place in the library, but Jordy himself does not hold an MLS degree. (The issue of nondegreed librarians in itself is an entirely different knee-jerk topic in the library field, which I won't be dealing with at length in this work.) Abbott's attention to the day-to-day minutiae—and problems—of a small-town public library reflect a very good working knowledge of libraries, and his characterizations are affecting, appealing, and grab you right off the bat. Although Jordy may not have had formal training in librarianship, he deals with all the same issues most public librarians and library managers do: staffing the circulation desk, answering difficult reference questions, providing a balance of materials to the patrons, funding allocations, and much more. The series gives readers insight into the challenges of small public libraries, and, as always, anything that shines a realistic light on the wide variety of responsibilities of librarians is welcome.

The Mobile Library Mystery Series, by Ian Samson

In the first of the Mobile Library Mystery series, *The Case of the Missing Books* (2006), we meet Israel Armstrong. Israel is a newly graduated librarian from

London and has accepted a posting as librarian to the small Irish town of Tumdrum. He has certain expectations about what his life will be like there, but these are immediately dashed upon his arrival. There's no one to meet him, no place for him to stay, and worst of all, the library is an empty shell of an abandoned building (closed by the Rathkeltair Department of Entertainment, Leisure and Community Services). So, he's assigned to run the bookmobile instead. Only problem is, there are no books—neither in the bookmobile nor in the library itself. And the bookmobile isn't called a mobile library anymore, but a mobile learning centre, and Israel isn't the mobile librarian, but is now the Outreach Support Officer. And ... the bookmobile has been used as a chicken roost for the last three years.

Israel Armstrong is not a happy man.

The local council arranges a spare room for Israel (with the chickens, on a farm run by a woman named George). Israel finds the council's implied threat of there being no library service for this corner of the country at all if he packs up and heads back to London more depressing than his current prospects, so he (despite his surly and antagonistic attitude) goes about trying to discover what happened to "his" books. This journey takes him all over the area, and he meets the inhabitants of the small town and surrounding county. Despite himself, he begins to learn what life is like in rural reality, how to get along with the locals, and the best way to deal with roosters in the morning; the ending is particularly charming.

The second in the series, *Mr. Dixon Disappears* (2006), is less a fish-out-of-water story than that of a fish-in-hot-water, as Israel (now comfortably ensconced as the mobile purveyor of books to the county, and no longer living with the chickens) becomes the prime suspect in the robbery of a department store and the disappearance of the store's titular owner. Suspended from his job, Israel discovers that Mr. Dixon was a member of an amateur magician's group; oddly, Dixon's family seems none too worried about either the robbery or the disappearance. In order to get his job back, Israel must solve the whole puzzle.

The third title in the series, *The Book Stops Here* (published in the U.K. as *The Delegate's Choice*), came out in August 2008. Israel finally gets to return home to London to attend a bookmobile convention, but then his is stolen. With the help of a friend from Tumdrum, Israel sets off to find his old but trusty bookmobile, all the while dealing with his mother, questions about his relationship with his long-distance girlfriend, whether he'll stay in Tumdrum, and an inadvertent trip to Stonehenge.

This series is off to a bit of a slow start, but remains interesting in that Israel's feelings of entitlement reflect the ongoing discussion in the library community about the position (and ranking) of MLS-holding librarians versus "paraprofessionals." While many of Israel's actions and statements could turn someone off to librarians, his desire to make sure everyone has access to a library is noble.

Also Worth a Look

Some other titles to consider are:

- *The Time Traveler's Wife*, by Audrey Niffenegger. The main character in this time-distortion romance, Henry de Tamble, is a librarian at the Newberry Library in Chicago. One of his memorable "chrono displacement" episodes involves a locked stairwell in the library, necessitating some fancy explaining.

- The Jacqueline Kirby series, by Elizabeth Peters. Jacqueline (friends call her Jake) Kirby is a librarian at a small college in the Midwest who keeps getting dragged into murderous situations. Even after becoming a successful romance writer, she always relies on her librarian skills for research and investigation.

- The Cat Who series, by Lillian Jackson Braun. Librarian Polly Duncan (and the Pickax library) features regularly in this cozy series centered on an ex-journalist and his detecting cats who live 400 miles from nowhere.

- The Discworld series, by Terry Pratchett. The Librarian of the Unseen University features in many of the Discworld stories; he was human once, but was changed into an orangutan by accident, and has no interest in being changed back. This has not in the least stopped him from performing his duties as librarian.

- *The Historian*, by Elizabeth Kostova. Librarians and libraries feature prominently in this widely traveled horror/mystery narrative; one of Dracula's goals is to find someone worthy of cataloging his extensive library, and much of the action goes on in various libraries around the world.

- *How I Fell in Love with a Librarian and Lived to Tell About It*, by Rhett Ellis. This short love story centers on a small town minister and the new librarian.

- *Here Lies the Librarian*, by Richard Peck. A young adult story set in the early years of the 20th century, about a young woman who loves cars and the librarian who changes her life.

Comics

Ah, the joys of library comics. We're lucky to have so many out there! This section describes some comics that feature librarians as main characters or are otherwise particularly relevant to librarians and libraries, but if you really want to get into the genre, check out Steven M. Bergson's webpages "Librarians in Comic Books" (www.ibiblio.org/librariesfaq/combks/combks.htm) and "Librarians in Comic Strips" (www.ibiblio.org/libraries faq/comstrp/comstrp.htm). And here's a fun little tidbit: Did you know that Superman's birth mother on Krypton was a librarian?

Unshelved,
by Gene Ambaum and Bill Barnes

"Welcome to *Unshelved,* the world's only daily comic strip set in a public library!" With that greeting, writer Gene Ambaum (a pseudonym) and artist Bill Barnes invite you into the world of the Mallville Public Library and all the wacky chaos contained therein. Ambaum is himself a librarian and the main writer for the strip (although both contribute ideas); many of the storylines start in real life—especially those that seem stranger-than-life. Asked in an interview about Ambaum's stories of working in a library, Barnes says: "They were filled with a vast array of strange characters doing disturbing things; bizarre situations rife with conflict. In short, endless opportunities for comedy" (www.comicbookresources.com/?page=article&id=11737). The two got together at a Comic-Con one year, and library humor history was made.

The main character, and our hero, is Dewey, the coffee-addicted, comics-loving YA librarian. The supporting librarian cast includes Tamara, the children's librarian, whose favorite letter is "T" and who holds a black belt in Aikido; Colleen, the techno-illiterate reference librarian, who has the entire card catalog memorized and loves it when the library's Internet access goes down; and Mel, the branch manager, who'd rather be browsing office supply catalogs. Most of the action centers around Dewey and his interactions with library-goers, especially with Merv, a school-avoiding, loves-the-library-but-hates-to-read technophile who idolizes Dewey; Buddy, originally a summer reading mascot but now a page at the library who never takes off his Book Beaver costume; and Cathy, a teacher at the high school and, despite Dewey's initial efforts, his unrequited love interest.

In and around these folks we see a constant stream of patrons and watch their interactions with the librarians and each other. Watching how each of the Mallville librarians deals with situations rings bells of truth for public librarians everywhere. Most issues faced by public libraries at some point show up in *Unshelved*. Be it censorship, free access to information, service availability, computer support, remodeling, book talks, the unsolvable reference interview, after-school homework help—one way or the other, Dewey and the gang address it.

Unshelved, by Gene Ambaum and Bill Barnes. Used with permission of Overdue Media LLC, www.unshelved.com.

In addition to the daily peek into life in the Mallville library, each Sunday Ambaum and Barnes write a "Book Club," where one of the characters talks about a book they've read and are recommending to a patron. (It should be noted that these books are, in fact, also read in full by at least one of the authors.) Done in full-sheet, full-color format, these are always interesting; as a way to do reader's advisory, this is a brilliant concept! These Book Clubs appear in libraries and independent bookstores across the nation, and the authors encourage their use to get the word out about good books. What's particularly cool is that featured authors have often contacted Ambaum and Barnes to let them know that they've enjoyed *Unshelved*'s summaries of their work.

Many kudos have been heaped on *Unshelved* for its unflinching, sometimes controversial, but always spot-on representation of life in a public library. Bravely, Ambaum and Barnes will have their characters say or do things that librarians everywhere wish they could do in real life, but wouldn't dare. As Barnes has said, "I get to draw Dewey saying the things everyone wishes they could say, except they'd be fired" (comicsworthreading. com/2007/02/21/congratulations-to-unshelved). In this way, these characters have become the outward expression of librarians' inner voices. Occasionally, the process comes full circle when a real life library does something first put forth in a comic. Once, for instance, Dewey was challenged to do something with the gum on the undersides of the tables in the teen area; he turned the table upside-down to create Gum Mosaic art. The children's librarian at Bayview/Anna E. Waden Library (San Francisco) ran with the idea to create an "Already Been Chewed Mosaic" kid's art program! Read *Unshelved* online at www.unshelved.com.

Rex Libris,
by James Turner

"Follow the story of Rex Libris, the tough-as-nails Head Librarian at Middleton Public Library, and his unending struggle against the forces of darkness. Wearing his distinctive, super-thick bottle glasses and armed with an arsenal of powerful weapons, he strikes fear into recalcitrant borrowers, and can take on virtually any foe, from loitering zombies to fleeing alien warlords who refuse to pay their late fees." Author and artist James Turner isn't kidding: In each issue, Rex faces off with some baddie or other over a library book, usually armed with a really large gun. He dreams of butter tarts and is known as "The World's Favorite Ass-Kicking, Sesquipedalian Librarian."

The Middleton Public Library isn't just any old library; it's the repository of all knowledge, known and unknown (both written books and ones only thought of can be found here, although the unreal books are kept in a secure area). And it doesn't just contain our knowledge here on Earth; this is a multidimensional, intergalactic kind of library. Charged by Thoth (the Egyptian god and the Administrator of the Library) with protecting the books, our hero sometimes has to go to extremes to do so. Backed up by fellow librarians Circe (the sorceress, now reformed) and Hypatia (recently granted her MLIS and an expert in close quarters combat), and hassled by roommate Simonides (a philosopher turned into a bird by Circe who wants to rule the world), Rex deals with everything from overdue books to patrons lost in the stacks. He speaks like an extra in a Sam Spade noir mystery, is almost never seen out of his dark suit and tie combo, and has a square head that is oddly appealing. (I did say I was a huge fan, didn't I?)

Issues in the series to date include:

- #1, "I, Librarian," where Rex deals with the demon spirit samurai Kurui-No-Oni, who wants to check out a book from the library but doesn't have a library card.

- #2, "Labyrinth of Literature," where Rex begins planning his trip to retrieve the overdue Principia Mathematica from the warlord Vaglox.

- #3, "Leap of Faith," where Rex and Simonides travel to Benzine V, home of Vaglox, and tangle with crystalline lifeforms.

- #4, "Battle on Benzine," where Rex continues his advance on Vaglox's stronghold, and Circe dispenses with some (literal) Vandals in the reading room.

- #5, "Tea with Vaglox," where Rex finally faces off with the warlord over his overdue book.

- #6, "Book of Monsters," where Rex must rescue a patron sucked into a dangerous tome of real and mythological monsters.

- #7, "Monster Merry-go-Round," where Rex continues his rescue mission in the Compendio Ilustrado.

- #8, "Escape from the Book of Monsters," where Hypatia finally gets to use some of her combat training, and Rex rescues the missing patron.

- #9, "In the Grip of OGPU!," where Rex takes us on a side trip down memory lane to a battle with the old Russian secret police over a luck-granting gem.

- #10, "A Cock & Bull Story," where Simonides re-enters the picture; Rex tries to convince Barry, his publisher, to share more of his life stories; and the librarians begin to prepare for the rising of R'lyeh.

- #11, "R'lyeh Rising," where Rex and a team of elite librarians join forces with a navy taskforce and head to the South Pacific to prevent Cthulhu from awaking and enslaving humanity.

- #12, "Space Balls … of Evil!," where Rex and his team face down a competing team of evildoers bent on gaining control of Cthulhu Two first. Circe is down; Rex is teleported away; can the good guys overcome?

- #13, "Convergence of Chaos," where Team Librarian is caught in a fierce battle for the world between the awoken Cthulhu Two's minions and Kronov's evildoers. Will Team Librarian survive?

Some notable quotes from the series:

- "Get Thoth a raspberry chocolate latte with the cream and chocolate sprinkles. Thoth commands, librarian! Obey! Sprinkles!" (This one almost made me spit coffee when I read it; Rex has just reported on his latest retrieval to the Boss, and Thoth is moping. He decides coffee is the solution to his mood.)

- "Just because I'm a librarian doesn't mean I'm at all tame."

- "Don't touch the dust! I have it all arranged." (This from Rex to Hypatia, who noticed the checkout desk looked new; it was destroyed the evening before by a cranky patron and took Rex all night to re-create.)

- "Thank God! Librarians!"

- "Now that is one tough librarian." (A personal favorite)

Also worth a mention—if I can do so without breaking any secret codes of silence—is Rex's involvement with the Ordo Bibliotheca (the International Order of Librarians). Founded in 242 BC in Alexandria, the Ordo Bibliotheca has

subtly guided civilization ever since, while protecting mankind from calamity and destruction (often with Rex leading the protection team). Rex is a long-standing member of high order; a little known fun fact is that Melvil Dewey is considered the greatest Archmagus of the Order. It should be noted that all librarians are considered to be members of the order, and "since at least the Sixth Century all librarians have received extensive combat training and are lethal with even the common toothpick." (Reader, keep this in mind the next time you feel like hassling the librarian behind the reference desk!)

It's undeniable: Rex is unlike any stereotype you've ever come across. The closest match is perhaps James Bond, but even he's not quite right. Rex always has a nifty tool or unexpected trick up his sleeve, his memory is encyclopedic, and he's quite fast on the draw. Unlike Mr. Bond, however, Rex is always on the lookout for more than just Number One—he has several times interrupted a high-priority mission to help a patron find a book or guide one out of the maze of stacks.

"With fists of steel and mind as sharp as a tack, Rex is a true guardian of knowledge, foe of the foolish, defender of the Dewey Decimal System, and the best hope for the future of civilization." Sadly, James Turner announced in October 2008 that Issue #13 will be the last one in the series, although he has not ruled out a return to Rex's world in the future. Learn more about Rex, Circe, Hypatia, and the Ordo Bibliotheca at www.jtillustration.com/rex.

Shelf Check,
by Emily Lloyd

Meet Jan. She's a reference librarian at a public library, who does her best to deal with her clueless boss Dave while juggling the often inane requests she gets from patrons. Creator Emily Lloyd—herself a librarian—skewers current library topics with humorous skill, covering everything from roving reference to censorship to ALA Read posters (her take on them has been a big hit with the ALA Read team), book displays, cultural and holiday displays, and even the social networking tools Facebook and Twitter. Jan is also out and proud, and is a tireless proponent for the GLBTQ (gay, lesbian, bisexual, transgender, and queer) community. She's even gone international in this area; when a man in Manchester, U.K., asked a gay librarian if someone else was available to help him, as he didn't approve of same-sex marriage, not only did Lloyd comment on the news site, she then had Jan address the issue in *Shelf Check* #113.

Shelf Check, *by Emily Lloyd. Image courtesy Emily Lloyd, shelfcheck.blogspot.com*

One of the nifty things about *Shelf Check* is the immediacy with which Lloyd has Jan respond and react to events and issues in the library world. For example, on November 30, 2007, library tech blogger David Lee King posted about adding a MeeboMe widget to his library's catalog (so that if a patron's search result came up empty, a chat window would pop up and link the patron directly with the librarian on duty). One week later, on December 7 (*Shelf Check* #152), Jan admits to Dave that she's engrossed in David Lee King's MeeboMe post, then has to convince Dave that it can't be used as a dating tool. Jan also addresses the issue of banned books with pointed humor; *And Tango Makes Three* has made several appearances, and a regular strip title is "Why Was I Banned?" (I had no idea that Shel Silverstein's work had been accused of promoting cannibalism!) As with *Unshelved*, sometimes it's nice to have a character who can say or do the things we all wish we could say and do in real life. Keep up and laugh or wince along with the stories of Jan's life in the library at shelfcheck.blogspot.com.

Barbara Gordon, Batgirl, and Oracle

We all know Barbara Gordon, aka Batgirl, was a librarian—but what happened next? She became Oracle, information broker to superheroes and a significant power herself. Barbara's life in comics is long and complicated. When we first met her back in the 1960s, she was Dr. Barbara Gordon, head of the Gotham City Public Library, and a more standard representation of librarians would be hard to find. Gordon sported frumpy clothes, large glasses, and bunned hair. She was quiet and unassuming, and we often saw her shelving books (which, of course, all directors of large public libraries have time in their schedules to do!). Batgirl went further than most superheroes to keep her secret identity safe—not only did she keep her identity as Barbara Gordon secret from her father, Commissioner Gordon, but she also kept it secret from Batman himself.

In the late 1980s, Batgirl had a significant and unfortunate encounter with The Joker, which left her paralyzed and in a state of depression. Exit, as they say, Batgirl. However, she "soon realizes that her aptitude for and training in information sciences have provided her with tremendous skills that could be deployed to fight crime"—and thus, Oracle is born. It is revealed that Barbara has "a genius-level intellect; photographic memory; deep knowledge of computers and electronics; expert skills as a hacker; and graduate training in library sciences." Who better to become the epitome of an information goddess in the superhero world? Oracle and her team, the Birds of Prey, remain active in comics today, interacting often with superheroes and police departments across the comic universe.

Oracle is widely noted as being the first librarian-as-superhero and is definitely a positive role model and anti-stereotype. Various people have been responsible for writing the stories of Batgirl and Oracle over the years, but comic book writer and editor Barbara Kesel (herself a tireless opponent of sexism in comic books) is credited with the most influence and responsibility for the rebirth of Batgirl as Oracle. One lovely side note: Kesel has a degree in library science!

Tom the Dancing Bug, by Ruben Bolling

Since 1990, Ruben Bolling (a pseudonym) has been skewering current events, modern life, politics, and a whole bunch of other things with his comic *Tom the Dancing Bug* (which features no bugs, no dancing, and no one named Tom). A banker in real life with a law degree from Harvard, Bolling includes a wide range of semi-regular characters in his intentionally unconnected strips, such as God-Man (whom he uses to discuss religion) and News of the Times (used to discuss current events). *Tom the Dancing Bug* has won the Best Cartoon award three times (and was a finalist two other times) since 2001 from the Association of Alternative Newsweeklies.

In 2000, Bolling used his News of the Times format to publish "Library System Terrorizes Publishing Industry," which met with a roar of approval from librarians across the nation with the proclamation that: "Mark my words: This 'Dewey Decimal System' will be the death of literature!" Interestingly—and just a bit depressingly—this comic seems just as relevant and appropriate today as in 2000. Given the current issues with digital rights management for music, with only a few modifications this comic would be just as powerful. Think also about ebooks; some digital readers restrict the enjoyment of a purchased ebook to a single user and require that the digital readers

Tom the Dancing Bug, *by Ruben Bolling.*
Image courtesy Quaternary Features.

TOM the DANCING BUG
PRESENTS:

by
RUBEN
BOLLING

of the

**Library
System
Terrorizes
Publishing
Industry**

A BOOK LOCATING/LENDING PHENOMENON KNOWN AS THE "**DEWEY DECIMAL SYSTEM**" – ENABLING USERS TO GET ACCESS TO COPYRIGHTED TEXT MATERIAL FOR FREE– HAS SENT SHOCKWAVES THROUGH A PANICKED PUBLISHING INDUSTRY.

WHY WOULD ANYONE **PAY** FOR A BOOK ONCE IT'S ACCESSIBLE **FOR FREE**?!

PUBLISHERS SPOKESMAN BRENT AULLETT

THE PLAN IS AS COMPLEX AS IT IS DIABOLICALLY CLEVER. A "LIBRARY" BUYS BOOKS, USERS FIND THEM THROUGH DEWEY'S CLASSIFICATION SYSTEM, AND BORROW THEM FOR FREE!

DIST BY UNIVERSAL PRESS SYNDICATE ©2000 R. BOLLING 5/0

THE INVENTOR OF THE SYSTEM IS **MELVIL DEWEY**, A PLUCKY 149-YEAR-OLD WHO'S BEEN DEAD FOR 69 YEARS, SO HIS BUSINESS PLAN IS UNCLEAR.

BUT HE'S GOT READERS GIDDILY BORROWING BOOKS, TO BE CONSUMED AT LEISURE, AND FREE OF CHARGE!

SCREW UPDIKE! I'M BEATING THE SYSTEM!

POWER TO THE PEOPLE!

ESTABLISHED WRITERS LIKE TOM CLANCY HAVE STOPPED PRODUCING THEIR OUTPUT.

WHAT'S THAT YOU SAY? **LIBRARIES**? FOR **FREE**?!

DENISE, GET ME OVITZ! I'M PACKING IT IN!

www.tomthedancingbug.com

YOUNG WRITERS HAVE ALSO GIVEN UP. BRAD McCLATCHEN HAS CEASED WORK ON HIS COLLECTION OF POEMS ENTITLED "OF AN OLEANDER, RECRIMINATE."

OBVIOUSLY, MY DREAM OF MAKING MILLIONS THROUGH POETRY IS DUST.

I'M CALLING MY BROTHER ABOUT THAT TIRE SALES JOB.

PUBLISHERS OF COURSE ARE SUING, BUT THEY ARE NOT OPTIMISTIC.

MARK MY WORDS: THIS "DEWEY DECIMAL SYSTEM" WILL BE THE DEATH OF LITERATURE!

NEXT: SHOWER–SINGING THREATENS MUSIC INDUSTRY!

I WANNA KNOW WHAT LOVE IS...?

not be shared. Let's hope that these challenges to libraries performing their mandate ease soon. Keep up with *Tom the Dancing Bug* at www.tomthedancingbug.com.

Frazz,
by Jef Mallet

Edwin Frazier, aka Frazz, is a songwriter (by desire) and janitor (by choice) at Bryson Elementary School. He's both a mentor to most of the kids there and a widely educated and knowledgeable man. In Jef Mallet's strip, which is often loaded with cultural references and nods to his personal interests (like cycling and running), we learn a lot about Frazz and why, although independently wealthy from his songwriting, he chooses to stay working as the janitor. His interactions with the students are both humorous and enlightening, as are his dealings with the teachers, and it's clear that Frazz values libraries. (He uses some of his songwriting money to purchase books for the school library, for example.) One story arc involves a school-endorsed "Get Lost in a Book" day, and it has become a tradition for Caulfield, the main student character, to choose a literature-themed costume every Halloween.

In this strip on September 18, 2004, with just one utterance ("Ah" can say so much), Frazz acknowledged both the librarian dilemma and the student's realization of it. If only it were a snap to let the whole world know about us and what we can do! (I also like that the featured librarian is a guy; there aren't a lot of guy librarians in pop culture these days.) Keep up with Frazz online at www.comics.com/comics/frazz.

Frazz, by Jef Mallett. © Jef Mallet/Dist.
By United Feature Syndicate, Inc.

Speed Bump,
by Dave Coverly

Dave Coverly's single-pane comic, *Speed Bump,* covers just about every topic imaginable; as he has said in interviews and on the *Speed Bump* homepage, "If life were a movie, these would be the outtakes." Back in 2001, he drew a wordless comic featuring a librarian that was such a hit and has been requested so often ("This cartoon generated so many positive responses from librarians …") that he's since turned it into a full-size color poster. This is one of those situations where the picture says a thousand words; with just one image Coverly sums up the problem librarians were facing (and still are) with the explosion of online information and provides one possible solution. Keep up with Coverly's unique outlook on life at www.speed bump.com.

Speed Bump, *by Dave Coverly. Image courtesy Dave Coverly.*

Also Worth a Look

Some other comics to check out include:

- *The Sandman*, by Neil Gaiman. *The Sandman* is an award-winning comic book series written by Neil Gaiman that ran from 1989–1996. It chronicles the adventures of Dream of The Endless, known as Morpheus, who rules over the world of dreams. Dream's domain is called the Dreaming; in the center of the Dreaming is Morpheus's home and also the location of the Library, presided over by Lucien, the Librarian. This library contains "all the books that have ever been dreamt of, including the ones that have never been written," and as such is a source of power and knowledge all its own. Several scenes throughout the 75-issue series are set in the library.

- *Turn the Page*, by Jayson. The cartoonist of this strip, identified by only a single name, creates four-panel stick-figure vignettes of life in a public library. They're often inspired by real-life events, which Jayson mentions in the blog postings attached to the comics. You can read them online at librarycartoons.blogspot.com.

- *Questionable Content*, by Jeph Jacques. The main character in this comic, Marten Reed, works in the local college library, and scenes are sometimes set there. Watch for them at www.questionable content.net.

- *Jack of Fables*, from DC Comics. In this world where fables are alive, Mr. Revise (the villain and Head Librarian of the Golden Boughs Retirement Center, in actuality a prison) leads a band of evil Librarians whose goal is to destroy the magic of the Fables. He causes some serious problems for Jack (of Little Jack Horner fame, now all grown up).

Movies

There's a larger group of movies featuring librarians in one way or another than you might expect. Here, I'll mention some of my personal favorites that highlight some of the common portrayals of librarians or that have influenced our perceptions of librarianship. For more, I recommend visiting "Librarians in the Movies: An Annotated Filmography," maintained by Martin Raish (emp.byui.edu/RAISHM/films/introduction.html) and "The Film Librarian," compiled by Steven J. Schmidt (www.filmlibrarian.info). A few movie goodies: Judi Dench, Tom Hanks, Helen Mirren, and Julia Roberts have all played movie librarians over the course of their careers.

The Mummy and Sequels

"I ... am a librarian!"

Thus states Evelyn Carnahan, the feisty heroine of the three *Mummy* movies (www.themummy.com). *The*

Mummy, released by Universal Pictures in 1999, introduces us to Evelyn (known as Evie) and her brother Jonathan, British residents of Cairo in the 1920s. Evie is the librarian at the Egyptian museum, while Jonathan is a no-goodnik gambler always on the lookout for the next big win. When he comes back from a card game with what seems to be a map to Hamunaptra, legendary city of the dead, he needs Evie's help to translate the hieroglyphics and help him find the city. To do so, they must engage the help of the man Jonathan "won" the map from, American adventurer Rick O'Connell. Adventure, drama, romance, backstabbing, and other liveliness (and deadliness) ensue as the map not only leads them and another band of treasure-seekers to the gold, but also raises the long-dead and not very nice wizard Imhotep. Evie's knowledge and keen grasp of information—and her ability to access said information while under attack—lets her, Rick, and Jonathan win the day.

The Mummy Returns, released in 2001, reunites our varied characters 10 years later in London, where Rick and Evie are now married with a son, Alex, who's even smarter than they are. Alex is kidnapped by Imhotep's henchmen, and the whole crew heads back to Egypt for a showdown. The third in the series, *The Mummy: Tomb of the Dragon Emperor* (2008) leaves Imhotep in the grave and takes us instead to the Far East, where Alex (now grown and an archaeologist) unwittingly awakens the millennia-dead Dragon Emperor, just as bent on world domination now as he was when he was cursed 2,000 years ago. Rick and Evie must come to his aid in order to once again save the world.

Unlike in the third movie, in the first two movies, it is Evie's knowledge and skill that ultimately provides solutions to the dilemmas the gang faces. Much as I enjoy these movies, though, after the first half of the first one the issue of Evie's librarianship pretty much fell to the wayside. The second movie makes only oblique references to it, such as when we see the large library she's established at her home in England. A promotional still for the third movie shows her standing in front of a filled bookcase, which seems to be a nod to the librarian aspect of the character, but that's the only nod there was. This bookcase turns out to actually be in a bookshop—because Evie is now a bestselling author. There's no nod to Evie being a librarian in the third movie, which continues the trend toward pure mummy action-adventure. However, that "I ... am a librarian!" line from the first movie is quoted to me so often that it obviously made an impact on the moviegoing public.

Read or Die!

Yomiko Readman is a quiet, unassuming young woman with a house full of books; at least, that's how she appears. In reality, she is The Paper, an agent of the British Library's Special Operations Division ("a group tasked to locating and protecting rare books worldwide") who is able to manipulate paper in any way while defending books (and knowledge) from those who would try to restrict them. The movie, an adaptation of a Japanese manga series by Hideyuki Kurata, tells the story of

Yomiko and her fellow agents' struggle against an evil mastermind who wishes to eliminate most of humanity using a lost symphony from Beethoven that supposedly causes anyone who hears it to commit suicide.

As with the *Mummy* movies, if you are expecting *Read or Die!* to deal with deep philosophical issues of librarianship, you'll be sadly disappointed. However, if you're up for a rollicking good yarn with a bibliomaniac at the center, not to mention librarians who save the world, then you're in for a treat!

Party Girl

An amazing number of people—men and women both— have told me that *Party Girl* was a huge influence in their decision to go to library school. By the time I gave my second talk on the topic of librarians and image and heard from another batch of folks with the same story, I figured it was time for me to watch the movie myself. Starring Parker Posey and released by Sony in 1995, the movie tells the story of Mary (Posey), a "free-spirited" woman whose life is filled with wild parties, drugs, and not much responsibility. When she's arrested one night, she calls her godmother to bail her out of jail; her godmother agrees on the condition that Mary gets a job to pay her back. Mary is unable to find a job on her own, so her godmother arranges for her to get a job as a clerk at the library where she works. Mary's destructive tendencies continue, however, until she loses both her job and her apartment; a long night spent hiding in the library brings an epiphany, and Mary begins to straighten out. The film ends with her decision to pursue library school.

Watching Mary move off the problem path she'd been on and decide to become a librarian, without losing any of her style or personality quirks, made for an enjoyable movie. I can see how it could be considered deeply influential, and I'm glad a popular comedy could show librarianship in such a positive way.

The Hollywood Librarian: A Look at Librarians Through Film

A serious documentary in the midst of all these fictional librarians, *The Hollywood Librarian* (www.hollywood librarian.com), created by Ann Seidl, herself a librarian from Denver, shows "the realities of 21st century librarianship, including stereotyping, censorship and intellectual freedom, and the total impact of librarians in our culture and society." It's the first full-length documentary film that focuses on the work and lives of librarians, as illustrated through popular American movies. Clips from dozens of films featuring librarians are shown and discussed, interspersed with interviews with dozens of real-life librarians about their lives and work. The documentary also discusses topics of interest to librarians everywhere, such as budget cuts, pay equity, and technology. The film premiered at the 2007 ALA Annual Meeting to generally positive reviews and has since been touring public libraries around the world. A DVD-for-purchase production of the film is underway.

Also Worth a Look

Some other movies you may want to view include:

- *The Gun in Betty Lou's Handbag.* Betty Lou is a quiet, mousy, unassuming librarian in a small town and is ignored by everyone, including her husband. That is, until she finds the gun used in a gangland murder—then she has everyone's attention! Starring Penelope Ann Miller and released in 1992, it's an amusing romp.

- *Black Mask.* Jet Li is a secret supersoldier who, after the project is disbanded, tries to live life quietly as Michael, a librarian. However, his former companions are living a different kind of life, and Michael is the only one who can stop them. (Originally released in Hong Kong as *Hak Hap* in 1996, re-released and dubbed in the U.S. in 1999.)

- *The Time Machine.* In this 2002 remake of the H.G. Wells classic, scientist-inventor Alexander Hartdegen (played by Guy Pearce) consults a librarian in the 2030 New York Public Library, who is actually a hologram named Vox (played by Orlando Jones) and is "the repository of all human knowledge."

- *The Day After Tomorrow.* In this apocalyptic climate change film from 2004, the young hero Sam (Jake Gyllenhaal) and his friends take refuge in the New York Public Library, along with others escaping the maelstrom outside. One of these people is a librarian; she objects when the group decides to start burning books for warmth and shows later that "books are good for more than just burning" when she uses a medical reference book to diagnose a problem with one of Sam's friends.

Music

Surprisingly, a lot of pop music is about or references librarians. Here's just a small sampling, and, yes, a little librarian-related music factoid: Tori Amos's 2003 best-of release is titled *Tales of a Librarian*. Amos says that, as librarians are chroniclers, this is the chronicle of her life—and the list of tracks on the CD is arranged in Dewey Decimal order.

BlöödHag

Let me introduce you to BlöödHag (www.bloodhag. com), an edu-core band who thinks you should read more. (You've got to love a band whose motto is "The faster you go deaf, the more time you have to read!") An educational heavy/punk/speed-metal band from Seattle, BlöödHag specializes in songs about science fiction and fantasy writers and their stories, each titled with the author's name. At their live shows, which are very popular in the Pacific Northwest, they throw (secondhand) books into the audience. Their most recent album, the

Blöödhag's Hell Bent for Letters *album cover.*
Art by Gene Ha; cover courtesy Alternative Tentacles Records.

2007 *Hell Bent for Letters*, has some great cover art. The
heroine in the center of the artwork—Librarian Barb
Ryan, according to her ID card—is a "rampaging librarian
warrior queen who has slain a group of men with overdue

notices and beheaded a goblin." She has the bun, she has the glasses—but she also has a sword with "Shh!" etched into the blade, and her knife sheath says "Read." Fabulous!

Haunted Love

"Librarian" by Haunted Love is the funniest, and possibly the creepiest, song about libraries and librarians I've ever heard! Set in a library, it shows two rather ... focused ... librarians and a young man who stands in for the "typical" librarygoer: chewing gum, folding page corners, listening to music. (I'm sure we're all familiar with this type.) As the subtitle states, "This boy has no understanding of library protocols." The two librarians come at him with the über-shush, inviting him into the reserved area with promises of being able to read the new magazines and touch the first editions. Sadly, it doesn't turn out quite that way. Watch the video online (and listen closely to the lyrics, they're quite a kick!) at www.youtube.com/watch?v= Ne_WXP7lUWM.

SNMNMNM

The North Carolina–based band SNMNMNM "has a deep love and appreciation for the Dewey Decimal System." Thus, the first song on their new album *Crawl Inside Your Head*, titled "Addy Will Know," is a tribute to librarians everywhere and their ability to find the answers to myriad questions. From their wiki (addywill know.pbwiki.com): "'Addy Will Know' avoids the stereotypes. Serving as a musical tribute to the modern librarian, it is about a real librarian who leads a lost patron to the four books he is looking for. The names of the books are never mentioned, but as a kind of puzzle, the song itself includes call numbers that correspond to the books hinted at in the verses. Since 'Addy Will Know' is essentially a song about you, the modern librarian, we want you to participate!" The band held a contest to identify these four books, and the first 10 librarians to correctly identify them won a copy of the new album. "Addy Will Know" is both a catchy tune and a great homage to the power of librarians! Learn more about SNMNMNM at www.myspace.com/snmnmnm.

My Morning Jacket

"Librarian" is a recent release from this Kentucky-based rock band (from the June 2008 album *Evil Urges*); it is described as a "sweet little ballad of desire," and you can hear it at tinyurl.com/3t46ny. The lyrics, though, feed smack into the stereotypical ideas, with lines like "simple little bookworm, buried underneath … is the sexiest librarian … take off those glasses and let down your hair for me." Even with that, it's become quite a popular song, with 3,565 listeners at Last.fm and multiple mentions across the blogosphere.

Cascada

Cascada's "Every Time We Touch" is a typical pop/dance song. While the lyrics could be classified as a standard "pining for you" love song, the video brings it all together. Set in a library, the object of the beautiful female singer's affection is a male librarian. He comes complete with glasses, bow tie (the male stereotypical equivalent of the bun), and shushing action, and, while she dances through the library singing of her longing for him, he's hustling about fixing the card catalog and looking dismayed at all the noise. The library patrons also start out by looking a bit put off when the singer jumps up on the reading table and goes to town, but then they all start dancing as well. Then, because we all know what happens when you take off a librarian's glasses and loosen his tie, the singer turns the librarian into a wild dancer, too! The video ends with a great scene involving all the library patrons dancing with the singer and librarian around the library; it's too bad that it plays into both the male librarian stereotype and that of the poor, repressed librarian! See the video online at www.youtube.com/watch?v=ZK0GmiSMNGI.

Television

From children's shows and supernatural series to action-adventure films and even a soap opera, we've seen a lot of great librarian portrayals on television over the past few years.

Rupert Giles

A central character of the long-running TV series *Buffy the Vampire Slayer*, Rupert Giles (often just Giles) was Buffy's Watcher, serving as both guardian and mentor. He worked as the librarian of Sunnyside High School for the first several seasons, and many strategizing sessions were held there. This was probably the only high school library on the planet with a detailed and thorough collection of books on the metaphysical and magical issues of hunting the forces of evil—which were critical to Buffy's success on her missions. As Xander, one of Buffy's friends, says about Giles: "He's like SuperLibrarian. Everyone forgets, Willow, that knowledge is the ultimate weapon."

Giles and Buffy were featured in the cover story of the September 1999 issue of *American Libraries*. The author of the article, GraceAnne DeCandido, writes that "perhaps only Katherine Hepburn in the motion picture *Desk Set* has done more for the image of the library profession than the character Rupert Giles on the television series *Buffy the Vampire Slayer*." Of course, Giles himself is impacted by the stereotype in a few ways—most noticeably, he's male as well as quite techno-challenged—but with his wit, wiles, skills, and intelligence he showed that a librarian can be, and do, anything!

Between the Lions

The PBS children's show *Between the Lions* (pbskids. org/lions) is set in a library and staffed by librarian lions.

American Libraries *cover from September 1999 featuring Rupert Giles. Cover courtesy* American Libraries.

Starring Theo and Cleo (the parents, also the librarians) and Lionel and Leona (the kids, learning about the library), each episode shows a wide variety of people and animals reading all kinds of books, using the library's resources, and asking the librarians for help. The series provides very positive portrayals of reading, libraries, using libraries, and librarians that can find anything at the drop of a hat. It's also written very cleverly, with a line or two in each episode that appeals to adults as well. This is quite possibly the best representation of librarians and libraries on TV today.

The Librarian Movies

In 2005, TNT released a made-for-TV movie called *The Librarian: Quest for the Spear*. Starring Noah Wyle as Flynn Carsen, a perpetual student finally booted out of school and into real life, *The Librarian* is an action-adventure series requiring a high level of "willing suspension of disbelief." Flynn is invited to apply for the position of the Librarian at the Metropolitan City Library; after an intimidating interview with Charlene (Jane Curtin), he's hired. Immediately, he learns that this position is more than he thought: The Librarian is charged with protecting the greatest relics and writings of history. So, of course, the museum is robbed of a particular relic, and Flynn is sent off to retrieve it. In this installation, the relic stolen is a piece of the spear used to pierce the side of Jesus Christ on the cross; whoever holds the entire spear can control the world's armies. Flynn must head into the jungles of South America, work out his partnership with another operative of the Library, and track down the missing pieces of the spear; in doing so, he exposes an ages-old evil brotherhood and saves the world. (Bob Newhart has an awesome action sequence in the final fight.)

In 2006, *The Librarian: Return to King Solomon's Mines* was released, with the same actors and same basic premise. This time, the secret to locating an unimaginable hoard of treasure—which just happens to hold a book that gives its reader ultimate power—is stolen. Flynn to the rescue, once more! This time, he heads to Europe and then across Deepest Africa (making excellent time on foot, I might note) to a mysterious holy mountain. In order to solve this mystery, he must connect with a beautiful archaeologist and face some of the mysteries of his own family. *The Librarian: Search for the Judas Chalice* was released in December 2008; this time, Flynn heads to New Orleans in search of a cursed cup also being sought by someone calling himself Prince Vlad Dracul. You know that if this chap gets hold of the Chalice, it won't end well for the world; Flynn must once more throw himself into harm's way and save the day.

These tongue-in-cheek (but entirely enjoyable) action-adventure romps give a significant nod to Indiana Jones, but have no actual connection to real-world libraries and librarianship. While the title character is called "The Librarian" and nominally works for a library, the electronic discussions that flew about after the premiere of the first movie made perfectly clear that these movies should be taken as pure entertainment and not a movie about "real" librarians. (For that, you should see *The Hollywood Librarian.*)

The Librarians

In late 2007, the Australian Broadcasting Company premiered a six-episode comedy-drama series called *The Librarians* (www.abc.net.au/tv/librarians), which was set in a library (the Middleton Interactive Learning Center). This first series was very well received, and a second is currently in the works. From the press release, it "centres on the trials and tribulations of Frances O'Brien, a devout Catholic and head librarian. Her life unravels when she is forced to employ her ex-best friend, Christine Grimwood—now a drug dealer—as the children's librarian. Frances must do all she can to contain her menacing past and concentrate on the biggest event of the library calendar—Book Week." Frances's staff is possibly the most dysfunctional library crowd ever encountered, and she herself has quite the abrasive personality. When she's not trying to discover who's putting odd items in the book return drop, preparing the library (and herself) for center stage at Book Week, coping with Christine's court dates, and trying to figure out her own relationships, Frances is alienating the local Muslim community, dealing badly with children on school holiday, and generally being the kind of manager you don't want to have. I'm looking forward to seeing what the next series is like!

The cast of Australian Broadcasting Company's
The Librarians. *Photo courtesy ABC TV Publicity.*

Advertising

In 2003, Jennifer Tobias gave a talk at the Special Libraries Association (and published an associated article in *Information Outlook*) titled "Ad-Lib: The Advertised Librarian." She spent five years studying the appearance of libraries and librarians in advertisements from around the world—and there are some doozies out there! Tobias shares a telling rule for advertisers from *American Libraries* in the 1990s: "Librarians should never be depicted as spinsters or 'little old ladies.' Male librarians do not ordinarily wear bow ties. Exaggerated breasts and buttocks, shushing lunges, and SILENCE signs are unacceptable in *American Libraries*." Seeing some of the international ads she obtained permission to show at the conference was educational as well as funny and depressing; for every depiction of culture, intelligence, and coolness, there was another depiction at the other end of the scale, showing buffoonery, cluelessness, and libraries as low-class. I recommend you check out her work. Looking at some of the advertising released in the U.S. in the last few years, I found that many of them play into the "repressed librarian" stereotype, but I'm glad to report that the tide is turning and more advertisements are starting to present librarians in a positive way.

In 2001, Honda released an ad for the new Accord model, with a picture of the car and text reading: "The automotive equivalent of a really hot librarian. Good-looking, yet intelligent. Fun, yet sophisticated. All in a very eye-catching, 200-horsepower package. The Accord V-6 Coupe." Well, you can imagine the discussions flying around the library mailing lists! Commenters were in one of two camps: those who were bothered by the back-handed positivity of the ad, and those who felt complimented by being compared to a sexy car. (My question at the time was, what about all the good-looking *and* intelligent, fun *and* sophisticated folks out there?) When I showed this ad at a conference presentation and did a quick survey of the room, it broke down about half and half, with a lot of laughter thrown in! View the ad at www.librarian-image.net/img02/honda_librariancar.jpg.

During the same time frame, Bacardi released a now-infamous (well, in library-land) ad featuring a back view of a scantily clad woman and the blurb "Librarian by day. Bacardi by night." On one hand, it's always nice to see something other than bunned hair and shushing; on the other hand, this plays so completely into the repressed and/or naughty librarian stereotype that it's scary. Needless to say, this was also a very hot topic on many electronic mailing lists; I received excerpts from pop culture lists, law library lists, public library lists, and scientific discussions. Years later, this is still a heavily utilized image on many blogs and websites, and the ad pops up in conversations fairly regularly. (I found blog postings discussing it as recently as April and May of 2008.) Bacardi, however, is well-known for releasing "*X* by day, Bacardi by night" ads featuring scantily clad people; I suppose it was only a matter of time before librarians joined the bankers, auditors, and even vegetarians who break free of their bonds and run amuck after a shot of rum. View the ad at www.librarian-image.net/img02/bacardi.jpg.

In 2002, Hewlett-Packard released an ad featuring Eugenie Prime, who was at that time Manager of Corporate Libraries for HP (she has since retired). The ad shows Prime in front of a giant pile of books, and its text reads: "What the Internet needs is an old-fashioned librarian. Finding what you want on the web should be as easy as finding a book in a library. It will be, if Eugenie has her way. She's working to create a standard for labeling and cataloging information online—including all 2.7 billion web pages—a virtual Dewey Decimal system, if you will. So you can spend less time looking for, and more time using, the information you need. Shh. You're on the Internet." This is definitely a positive portrayal of a modern librarian. I now understand that the way in which she is presented acts as a bridge between the old/familiar and the new/technological, but at the time I really wished that she had been presented in a less stereotypical way than "old-fashioned librarian" (she's wearing that infamous twin set and pearls). View the ad at tinyurl.com/6dvtqd.

In 2006, DHL (the delivery service) ran a television ad during the World Series showing a DHL deliveryman pushing a loud, squeaky hand truck through a large library (so quiet, you can hear the church bells chiming). Almost immediately, he is loudly shushed by the old, cranky-looking, bespectacled and be-cardigan'd librarian, so he picks up the boxes and leaves the hand truck behind. Of course, then his shoes begin loudly squeaking. Patrons are looking on with mixed expressions of amusement and annoyance as he creeps across the floor with his boxes; when he reaches the reference desk, we see that he's taken off his shoes. (View the ad at www.youtube. com/watch?v=tz8L0oLIyak.) It's amusing as these things go, but plays right into the stereotypes. I personally like Brian Smith's suggested alternate ending (www.laughing librarian.com/2005_10_01_archive.html): "The shushing librarian says to the delivery guy, 'Yeah, it's great that you stopped rolling that noisy hand truck and took off your squeaky shoes. Now get these boxes off the reference desk, take them back to your truck, and deliver them to the service entrance.'" (Laughing Librarian, indeed!)

In 2007, Sony launched a series of ads for its digital book reader, called the Sony Reader. In giant wall posters, on the fronts of staircase steps, wrapped around support columns, and in myriad other places, Sony's ad read, in total: "Sexier than a librarian. The Reader. From Sony." From the airport at LAX to the BART floors in San Francisco to the subways of NYC, this ad was plastered all over the place, and librarians took notice in a big, big way. The uproar was so loud that Sony actually changed its advertising campaign and admitted on the Sony Electronics Blog that the original intent was "playing off a certain stereotype or a fantasy, depending on how you look at it." Later ads were amended with "(your librarian may vary)." Let's hear it for a mass uprising! View the ad and read discussion about it at www.flickr. com/photos/albaum/1356519239, and then read Sony's response at news.sel.sony.com/electronicsblog/?p=23.

Toys and Tees

Toys? Librarians don't have toys! Ha, I say. Not only do many librarians collect toys and other quirky bits of librariana, we even have our own action figure, resplendent upon many a desk. And tees? As in T-shirts? Yeah, sure, pull the other one: Librarians only wear twin sets or dowdy suit jackets. If you still think so after reading through all of this, you'd be wrong: Not only are we wearing tees, we're designing them. Read on to learn more.

The Librarian Action Figure

You would have to be living under a rock not to have heard of Nancy Pearl and the Librarian Action Figure (LAF) modeled after her. Brought out by quirky toymaker Archie McPhee (www.mcphee.com) in 2003, this has generated more discussion by librarians than just about any other librarian representation in popular culture. The LAF (www.mcphee.com/laf) has even outsold the Jesus Action Figure on the Archie McPhee website! There are now two versions available. The original came in a blue dress-and-cardigan combination, with a stack of books and Amazing Shushing Power! It was so popular that Archie McPhee released a deluxe version two years later, including two new stacks of books, a book cart, and a backdrop of a library, reference desk, and computer. The deluxe version also came in a cranberry red outfit—but still had that Amazing Shushing Power!

The Librarian Action Figure (deluxe edition).
Image courtesy Archie McPhee.

The whole thing started over dinner, wine, and a discussion of the Jesus Action Figure between Nancy Pearl and the owner of Archie McPhee, in which they decided that a librarian action figure would fill a certain niche. As Pearl explained in an interview on LISNews, "The people who perform miracles every day are librarians" (lisnews.org/node/15750). They decided Pearl herself should be the model, because she didn't take herself too seriously. In the LISNews interview, she noted that the action figure will show "which librarians have a sense of humor." When Archie McPhee brought out the original version, word spread like wildfire through librarian communities. From newspaper articles to email lists, comments seemed split pretty evenly between "love it" and "hate it." Media sources of all types picked the story up and ran with it: A librarian in Sidney, Australia, was quoted in the *Sidney Morning Herald* as saying "The shushing thing just put me right over the edge," while CNN got in on the story with an article titled "Librarians Oppose Shushing Action Figure," and NPR interviewer Melissa Block referenced "librarian rage" in an interview with Pearl. At the same time, a few comics ran strips on the topic; on October 13, 2003, *Overdue* (now *Unshelved*) asked "What if every superhero read the same book?," and *Stone Soup* (on November 2, 2003) went with "It's a man ... a woman ... it's ... Action Figure Librarian!"

When asked on LISNews about the negative reactions to the action figure, Pearl replied, "The LAF isn't real; it's great that the profession has attracted many different sorts of people, and continues to do so [...]" In a later interview with Margaret Fast, Pearl said that "it pleases me no end that the LAF shows that librarians are able to laugh at themselves, and not take themselves too seriously" (www.habitsofwaste.wwu.edu/issues/7/iss7art3a.shtml). In a time when intellectual property, privacy, and information access issues are at the forefront of the news so often, she notes, it's also important to remember that we may laugh at ourselves, but that we do take our "responsibilities to the public seriously, and take Intellectual Freedom issues very seriously indeed." Well said, Nancy!

Questionable Content

The online comic strip *Questionable Content* was briefly mentioned earlier, and its artist, Jeph Jacques, often creates novel T-shirts for each of the characters in the strip to wear. When he gets a response from his readers about wanting the design in real life, he'll actually create one and make it available for purchase. The shirt that has received the most attention in the library world is "She Blinded Me with Library Science," a nod both to musician Thomas Dolby and to the main character's work in the college library. You can get one for yourself at questionablecontent.net/merch.php.

Rex Libris

In addition to his great *Rex Libris* comics, James Turner has put out two Rex Libris T-shirts. Shirt #1 shows the seal of the Ordo Bibliotheca; shirt #2 features a great little shot of Rex from the front, pointing, with the slogan "Have YOU Returned Your Library Books?" Turner also designed and created a limited-edition release of a 6.5 inch statue of Rex, in combat pose, "featuring the librarian stomping on the severed hand of a demon who had one too many overdue books." In the spirit of full disclosure, I must admit I own all three of these items ... having Rex on my desk (next to my Librarian Action Figure, of course) just brings a certain something to my office. Buy your own at www.slgcomic.com/James-Turner_c_56-1.html.

"She Blinded Me with Library Science" T-shirt image from Questionable Content. *Image courtesy Jeph Jacques, questionablecontent.net*

Other Stuff

The explosion of the Internet, along with affordable options for create-on-demand items, has provided a shopper's playground for anyone looking for library- or librarian-themed things. You can choose from T-shirts, mugs, buttons, bags, even underwear—just visit

CafePress (www.cafepress.com) and make your choice. According to a recent themed ad for CafePress, there are more than 15,000 items available related to librarians—it makes the head spin!

Library calendars, though, are not as generally available from the create-on-demand shops. Calendars seem to fall into two categories: library calendars, such as the breathtaking, gorgeous Renaissance Library Calendar released every year (www.renaissancelibrary.com), and librarian calendars. In most cases, and somewhat notoriously, the librarian calendars feature (apparently) nude librarians with strategically placed books or other library impedimenta. So far librarians in California (2003), Canada (2003), London (2004), Wisconsin (2006), and Texas (2007–2008) have all posed for fundraising calendars. Who knows who'll appear next?

I can't let this chapter close without mentioning Conan the Librarian! By now you've probably run across this little pop culture librarian meme at least once before; he's probably been around nearly as long as Robert Howard's original Conan the Barbarian. The first known appearance of Conan as the Librarian was in a Canadian children's show called *You Can't Do That on Television* in 1982. My first exposure to him was in a *Mother Goose and Grimm* comic from 1987, where a grim-faced muscular librarian waits for a late return behind an "Overdue Books" sign; he's also appeared on *Reading Rainbow* and even has his own Mac software program that shushes the user if the sound coming through the speakers exceeds a certain volume. (Just what we've always wanted, a shushing barbarian librarian!) One of the most (in)famous appearances of Conan the Librarian was in Weird Al Yankovic's 1989 movie *UHF*, where the camera pans across a library to a large, muscled, fur-wearing, sword-wielding man while the announcer says, "Never before in the history of motion pictures has there been a screen presence so commanding, so powerful, so deadly—he's Conan the Librarian!" As a patron asks for help finding a book, the librarian picks him up by the collar and asks, "Don't you know the Dewey Decimal System?" (tinyurl.com/2pwvwt). Believe me, this is not a librarian you want to be late returning your books to!

Dozens of librarians identify themselves as "Conan the Librarian," including a contestant on Jeopardy, several bloggers, some folks at LiveJournal, some on MySpace, and at least one in Second Life. Conan is also the star of a series of adventures from the library staff at the William Mitchell College of Law (tinyurl.com/jq7r): "He inhabits the mythical Information Age, where he is a typical reference librarian. His world nevertheless bears some strange similarities to our own." The first series is sadly lost to the mists of time; the second series, "The Return of Conan the Librarian," and third, "Conan the Librarian on the Information Highway," hold a lot of amusement for librarians. A common theme runs through a lot of these representations: I'm sure at one time or another we've all wanted to take a giant sword to problematic patrons—and Conan allows us to enjoy that fantasy. This is an image that just won't die! I'm sure it's only a matter of time before the online multiplayer game "Age of Conan: Hyborian Adventures" (brought to you by the same people who created Second Life) has a reference library—appropriately staffed, of course.

Graphics and Permissions

Page 22: Covers of *Miss Zukas and the Library Murders* and *Index to Murder* courtesy of Avon Books.

Page 25: Cover of *The Librarian* courtesy of Nation Books.

Page 27: *Do Unto Others* cover copyright © 1994 by Random House, Inc. Used by permission of Ballantine Books, a division of Random House, Inc.

Page 33: The *Unshelved* logo is used with permission of Overdue Media LLC, www.unshelved.com.

Page 36: *Rex Libris* image courtesy James Turner.

Page 39: The great seal of the Ordo Bibliotheca image courtesy James Turner.

BREAKING THE STEREOTYPE

You see, I don't believe that libraries should be drab places where people sit in silence, and that's been the main reason for our policy of employing wild animals as librarians.

—Monty Python, *Gorilla Librarian* (1969)

I have met so many cool people since I became a librarian! Not just at conferences but on planes, hiking up mountains, even standing in lines at a pie joint; we're truly everywhere and do everything. As part of the research for this book, I was honored and delighted to interview modern librarians around the world about their jobs, their hobbies, and their lives as librarians. In this chapter, we're going to meet them and learn how they, in their everyday work and life, bust out of the stereotypical librarian role. I'll also talk about some other librarians and groups that do the same thing, some of whom are dedicated completely to the "anti-stereotype" of librarians.

Today's Librarians

In my travels around the country, both for my job and for leisure, I often find myself in conversations with people about librarians, libraries, and librarianship. There's not much middle ground between "Holy cow, you wouldn't believe what librarians do today!" and "Sure, I get help at the library all the time." The librarians featured in this chapter are doing their best to shift more people into the first mind-set. (Since their careers span time, space, and specialties, we'll stick with a tried-and-true alphabetical listing.) Note that it's not just public librarians that are involved in this public education effort; I was pleased to interview astronomy, business, law, mathematics, and technology librarians as well. We truly are everywhere! While each of the librarians I interviewed has a different background, different specialty, and different focus, and uses different skill sets to provide information to his or her patrons, there's also a lot of similarity across the board. Each uses the tools at his or her disposal to educate their patrons—and anyone else they encounter—as to who librarians are, what we can do, and why they need us.

Stephen Abram

Stephen Abram is a special librarian based out of Toronto, Ontario, Canada—although he is never there; he can primarily be found traveling the world, talking about libraries and librarianship. In his mid-50s, Stephen's official job titles are

Vice President for Innovation at SirsiDynix (a vendor of library software solutions) and Chief Strategist for the SirsiDynix Institute. As of 2008, he was also President of the Special Libraries Association (SLA; www.sla.org). When asked what he really does, Stephen gives multiple answers, as so many of us do. In addition to traveling the world giving speeches, keynotes, and workshops, he does research on user and librarian behaviors, meets with client executive teams to give advice and facilitate conversations about future strategies, and writes on these topics in articles, columns, and books. He labels himself a "futurist," and as part of his work and research, he uses every type of web-based "2.0" tool you've ever heard of—and, no doubt, some you haven't. He's a tireless pusher of the idea of playing to learn, which doesn't just mean gaming in libraries, but also involves giving yourself permission to play with tools in order to learn how to use them and to see how they could be used by your library or your patrons. One of his efforts as SLA President was the implementation and rollout of the SLA Innovation Laboratory, a centralized and secure playground for all kinds of web-based and interactive tools where SLA members can experiment and learn.

Stephen came to his analysis of libraries and librarians honestly: His undergraduate degree is in anthropology. He, like all of us, hears random comments about the profession: "You're not like any librarian I've met!" or "I've never heard of an MLS doing your type of work!" or "Why would a software company need a librarian?" He's been pretty tireless in answering that question and explaining why MLS holders *do* do this type of work. On his blog,

Stephen's Lighthouse (stephenslighthouse.sirsidynix.com), Stephen writes about technology in libraries, Internet usage, social networking and social learning, Web 2.0 and Enterprise 2.0, and gaming—and these are just his most recent topics. He's very vocal about pushing for change and illuminating the varied and diverse skills and abilities of librarians. Anyone who's out there doing that gets a star in my book.

Amy Buckland

Amy Buckland is a brand-new librarian from Montreal, Québec, Canada. From a background in political science, she's now a Librarian in Library Technology Services in the McGill University Library and spends a huge amount of time being virtual. In 2007, Amy initiated McGill's presence in Second Life (SL); she is currently working hard on expanding that presence. She also looks at new technologies to see if and how they can be implemented in her library. The newer technologies currently in use at McGill, in addition to SL, include QuestionPoint chat reference, MeeboMe widgets, RSS feeds for events, and some great video tutorials. Her library has recently built a "Cybertheque," a "wifi zone of the library with 150 computers, a bajillion laptop plugs, super comfy sitting areas, and these amazing study pods that have a big screen you can plug your laptop into (or use the one supplied), a whiteboard for brainstorming, and are completely soundproof. Collaborative spaces with high tech capabilities are crucial for students and the library is the best place to have these spaces." It certainly sounds like an amazing space to me!

In her early 30s, Amy gets comments about being a librarian "all the frickin' time!" To quote, "In grad school I would constantly hear 'you need a master's degree to check out books/shush people?' and 'where's your bun?' and to be honest, for the longest time I couldn't tell people that I was going to be a librarian without laughing. When I start talking about all the technology I know about, people are genuinely surprised that a librarian would know this stuff. And I joke pretty often about books as a way to stir things up with people and make them realize that librarians deal with *all kinds* of information, not just what is printed and bound." Even though she's a relative newbie to the librarian scene, Amy has been agitating for libraries and librarians for much longer; she's been attending SLA conferences since 2006 and was McGill SLA Student Unit President in 2007. In between her time as Jambina Oh, SL Reference Librarian at Info Island International, and her work in Library Technology, she also manages to editorially coordinate the *Journal of Applied Psycholinguistics* for Cambridge University Press and is the publisher and editor-in-chief of *Library Student Journal*. In addition to SLA, she's a member of the American Library Association (ALA; www.ala.org), Canadian Library Association, and Québec Library Association. Oh, and she was, not entirely surprisingly, a *Library Journal* Mover & Shaker in 2008. No one will ever be able to accuse Amy of standing still. She's out there in front of her patrons in a multiplicity of spaces, doing her thing and showing by example that a librarian darn well *can* know about things like Second Life.

Laura Carscaddon

Laura Carscaddon is an academic librarian with a history background, based at the University of Arizona (UA) Libraries in Tucson, Arizona. Her title is Assistant Librarian, but that doesn't come close to covering what Laura does. Her subject specialties alone make my head spin; she has duties to the Accounting, Business Communication, Economics, Entrepreneurship, Finance, Management & Organizations, Marketing, and MIS departments. To simplify things for her students, she calls herself the Business Librarian.

When I asked Laura, who's in her mid-30s, what it was she really did in her job, just her answer made me tired! Her tasks vary day by day and can change based on what projects she's working on. She could "end up directly supervising student workers or working with an intern from the library school here on campus. Maybe at some point I end up in charge of a grant project and have to pay attention to grant fund management." Right now her job includes working with business students at different levels; evaluating resources (print and electronic), including selection and deselection; in-person bibliographic instruction for classes; developing scalable instruction tools that can be re-utilized; working on internal library projects such as "Friday Socials," a series of workshops introducing Web 2.0 tools to the staff; working with faculty, from helping with research to technology questions with the course management system; research and professional involvement (Laura is on the Marshall Cavendish Award Committee, one of the ALA-NMRT committees, this year); training library staff on business resources and databases; and exploring new technologies for their usefulness to the library.

Laura has started a blog, Researching @ Eller (blog.ltc.arizona.edu/researchingateller), for the Eller College of Management students, sharing various business research tools and information for the students. She also recently set up a UABizLib Twitter account and has just started advertising it to students. The UA library provides a chat reference service; it's staffed whenever the reference desk is, currently 24 hours a day, 5 days a week. In late 2007 Laura used SlideShare (slideshare.net) to demonstrate resources available to Executive MBA students, and it was a great success, with more than 200 viewings in the first week. To build on that success, she is creating additional slidecasts that she'll not only be able to share directly with the students, but also embed in the blog or within a class guide.

At her first job, Laura was quite often mistaken for a student when she worked at the reference desk and was often faced with the "You have a master's degree to do this?" question. Remember the story in Chapter 1 about the man who wanted the librarian to type up his son's school paper? That came from Laura.

Andrew Evans

Andrew Evans is an Academic Law Librarian at the Washburn University School of Law in Topeka, Kansas. He's the Head of Reference and Government Documents Librarian, and, like Laura, his answers to my question of what he really does at work just exhausted me. Here is his answer (and I quote):

- "I lead strategic planning for instructional and reference services, actively participate in library administration under the general direction of the law library director, attend law school department head meetings in the associate director's absence, supervise librarians in reference activities, and coordinate the faculty liaison program.

- "I create, develop, and teach specialized topics in advanced legal research courses. This includes being involved with getting a new one-credit subject-specific advanced legal research course approved by the law school's curriculum committee.

- "I schedule a reference desk staffed by eight librarians and two paraprofessionals providing 86 hours of coverage per week, supervise one full-time paraprofessional and 1–2 student workers, conduct meetings on reference strategic planning, establish a legal reference strategic initiative to integrate the law library into all areas of the law school, train part-time professional reference librarians, coordinate work and reference schedules of part-time librarians, approve work schedules, evaluate employees, and serve on a hiring committee. The law library uses Trillian at the reference desk to support various instant messenger (IM) clients.

- "I design and implement collection development policy for government documents and reference desk areas by assessing the needs of faculty, staff, students, and other patrons. I focus on improving collection development processes (e.g., identify structural, procedural, and physical limitations, interdepartmental frictions, conflicting priorities, and needs for space and equipment).

- "I assist the Director of the Legal Analysis, Research and Writing program by teaching individual classes on legal research, producing broadcast quality legal research training videos, advising LARW professors on appropriateness of topics for briefs, and helping select instructional materials. I teach legal information literacy to groups and individuals, provide in-depth research for faculty, and provide directional and "how to" research tips for law students and pro se patrons. I use PBwiki for my Advanced Legal Research class (washalr.pbwiki.com) and have students post assignments on that. (One student actually showed an assignment he worked on to a potential employer and got the job.)

- "I provide legal research, technology, and software training for the law school community. These training sessions include federal and state legislative history, subject-matter services, free legal research on the Internet, use of courtroom technologies, MS-Word, MS-PowerPoint, law library orientation, and effective use of email. I help maintain teaching technology and application software in classrooms. I troubleshoot student, staff, and faculty hardware and software problems.

- "I manage and maintain our federal government depository library program including training and managing employees in the department, making presentations at the state and national level, coordinating library outreach and promotion through campus events, and providing leadership to the government documents community with membership on committees.

- "I also help create and maintain sections of the WashLaw legal web portal (www.washlaw.edu) through the use of HTML, Dreamweaver, and HomeSite."

In addition to his time spent at the library, Andrew owns and runs a part-time martial arts school. "When students feel comfortable enough and work up the courage, they sometimes ask me what my day job is. Upon finding out I'm a librarian, they shake their heads in disbelief and say, 'You don't look like a librarian.' It takes a while, but I eventually convince them I am really a librarian." In his late 30s, he's also the founding member of the Butt-Kicking Librarians; read on to meet them later in this chapter.

Abigail Goben

Abigail Goben is a Youth Services Librarian for the La Crosse (WI) Public Library and came to libraries via a degree in English. She effortlessly combines the traditional and the modern in her job, including story time, reference desk work, after-school outreach programs (such as card games with teens and knitting classes), both children's and teen's summer reading programs, and collection development and management for the children's and young adult collections. In addition, she edits the library's monthly newsletters and coordinated a Knitting in Public Day—a one-day event spanning eight hours and attracting more than 300 attendees.

Abigail has become the Children's Department go-to person for both the library's web designer and the Head of IT/Technical Services. She's developing a MySQL database for the library's new website, only one of many that she'll design and develop; created the children's section of the new staff wiki; is writing training material on new intranet features; and will handle blog and website updates when the new site goes online in the fall of 2008. She also does staff technology training; her first sessions were on using OverDrive. Since the library is in a transition period with technology, its librarians have done some serious thinking about embracing social networking. Right now, the adult reference desk handles chat reference with Meebo, and the library has a Flickr account; the librarians also organize a very well-attended gaming program three days a week. (It was so well attended that it had to be restricted to teens only, as they were overcrowded to the point of being unsafe. Future plans include gaming events for adults and younger children.) Additional projects currently underway include a staff wiki, an online staff locator, and internal blogs; as part of the broader web redesign, RSS feeds for new books and blogs for the Children's, Teen's, and Adult departments will launch. The library will be moving to online registration for story times (which are also very well attended) and hopes to add videos and podcasts as time goes on.

Oh, to be so young (Abigail is in her mid-20s) and to have heard so many bad lines about being a librarian. Abigail has been hit with every cheesy line you've ever come across:

- "You're too young to be a librarian." (From Abigail: "Dissatisfied with the answer I'd given her, the patron demanded to know 'Who's in charge?' and was really thrown when I answered that I was.")

- "You're a librarian!? Wow, I've always had a fantasy about that." (From Abigail: "Whether it's a comment about how antiquated my profession is, how I must love to shush people, or how they want to see me 'with my hair down,' it's always an incredibly stupid insult.")

- "Librarians do that?" (From Abigail: "Once in a while, it throws them when they realize that checking out books is only in my job responsibilities under 'other duties as assigned.'")

- "You must get to read a lot." (From Abigail: "I hear this one a lot in conversation. I laugh at it.")

- "You don't dress like a librarian." (From Abigail: "One of my favorite things to say to reluctant parents in a story time is, 'Grownups, come on—if I can do "Head, Shoulders, Knees, and Toes" in three-inch heels, you can do it in sneakers.'")

Amy Hale-Janeke

Amy Hale-Janeke is a law librarian for the Fifth Circuit Court of Appeals Law Library in New Orleans, Louisiana (www.lb5.uscourts.gov). As Head of Reference Services, she primarily fulfills research requests—which can be as complex as compiling a legislative history, or as simple as finding a particular article for law clerks, judges, and staff attorneys. Last year, she fulfilled a research request for the newest Chief Justice of the United States, John Roberts. While, as Amy says, "the law likes to move sloooowly," much of what she does is electronic: She maintains an internal blog about news and events pertinent to the Fifth

Circuit and its judges, manages Westlaw and Lexis e-access, creates topic-specific intranet pages, and composes and distributes the Circuit's electronic newsletter twice monthly. She is also in charge of public relations, coordinates reference projects for all nine branches, sets up continuing legal education programs for the staff attorneys, and gives tours of the historic courthouse where the library is located.

Amy has also been hit with many of the "standard" lines about being a librarian. She's been told she has "too much personality to be a librarian, whatever that means," and has definitely run into the "you don't look like a librarian" comments. Now in her mid-30s, she says, "On my first professional library job, I decided to wear my contacts instead of my glasses for my first week. That turned out to be a mistake. All week, I watched as patrons approached my colleague, a nice white-haired gentleman with glasses, with questions. Even though I'd say, 'I can help you down here,' I was met with small frowns and head shakes from patrons. I chalked this reluctance up to the fact that I was new and looked young. That weekend, though, I decided to try an experiment on Monday morning. I decided not to wear my contacts. Instead I'd wear glasses and twist my hair up into a clip. It wouldn't be a bun, but it'd be close. Sure enough, when the library opened on Monday, people started asking me questions. I guess I finally 'looked like a librarian' to them and they felt comfortable approaching me." Outside her job at the library, Amy teaches belly dancing; when she tells people "I am a librarian by day, they are surprised. But then I whip out the bibliography of belly dance books and music and suddenly they can see my librarian peeking through."

Jill Hurst-Wahl

Jill Hurst-Wahl is a special independent librarian in her early 50s based in Syracuse, New York. She is President of Hurst Associates, Ltd. (www.hurst associates.com) and a librarian, but describes herself as more of an Information Consultant. With a background in the arts, competitive intelligence, and information technology, Jill describes her job as connecting people and their content to the world; Hurst Associates travels around the country working with cultural heritage organizations and multitype consortia to understand their digitization needs. This includes running workshops on digitization and copyright, conducting membership surveys for input, and giving presentations on social networking tools so that organizations can better understand their uses. Jill is now as well known for social networking as she is for digitization!

A tireless proponent of those social networking tools, Jill has become especially known for her work with Second Life. Her first foray into SL was intended to enable her to talk briefly and knowledgeably about it in workshops; that led to an interview about SL, which led to further exploration of SL, and, as Jill says, "the rest is history." Her in-world persona, Jillianna Suisei, can most often be found on Info Island, teaching and sharing information about SL. Jill now gives workshops and presentations just on SL and teaches a graduate level course on SL and Librarianship for Syracuse University. She says, "What was supposed to be fun has become a part of my business." Because of this, and the fact that Jill doesn't have patrons per se, she uses many, many tools to connect with colleagues and clients, including Facebook, Twitter, Meebo, Skype, blogs, and wikis. Jill says, "The more places I am, the better," and notes that she's gotten many leads through social networking tools that lead to conversations—and clients—in the real world.

Jill reports, "I sometimes have had business people say to me 'A librarian would be good at what you do' and then I tell them I am one!" She tries not to look like a "classic librarian" but leans more toward coming across as a businesswoman ("Keep in mind that libraries are businesses, too."). She now deals with the next level of image and perception, where it matters not at all what your avatar looks like in SL as long as you can provide the information.

Jill Jarrell

Jill Jarrell is a Teen Services Librarian in her late 20s, working at the Pikes Peak Library District in Colorado Springs, Colorado (library.ppld.org). She loves her job, which requires her to interact with teenagers on a daily basis; she manages the East Teen Center, which includes supervising work-study students and teen volunteers, policy management for the teen public desk, collection management, and programming support. She organizes the summer reading programs, in which typically 5,000 teens participate; provides ideas to the webmaster for the Teen Zone website; envisions and implements long-term improvements to teen services; provides homework help; does reader's advisory; and troubleshoots the video game consoles (including a PS2, PS3, Xbox 360, and Wii)—all of this on top of competing with the teens on Gaming Night, and reassuring parents!

Jill interacts with her teen patrons in various ways: the teen center has a blog (library.ppld.org/blogs/teen), a message board (www.websitetoolbox.com/tool/mb/teen zone), and a MySpace page (myspace.com/pikespeak libraryteens). In addition, Jill is implementing IM, runs video contests on YouTube, and has a Teen Booktalking Podcast (ppldbooktalks.podbean.com). She and her staff regularly host gaming nights, both for teens only as well as for teens and their parents, and they have a mobile game set with a PS2 and flat-screen TV that travels around to the 13 branches of the library system.

Most of the comments Jill gets from her patrons are very positive, such as the line we all love to hear: "This is an excellent library!" Occasionally she's mistaken for a teen volunteer, but has been able to reassure patrons that yes, she is the librarian. She says, "Mostly, patrons are just surprised that librarians do other work when we are not on the reference desk." Jill loves her job and loves surprising her patrons with the varied ways the library provides service.

J. Parker Ladwig

J. Parker Ladwig is an academic librarian at the University of Notre Dame (UND) in Indiana (www.library.nd.edu). In his early 40s, he is the Mathematics and Life Sciences Librarian; his responsibilities at two branch libraries (one for mathematics, excluding computer science, and one for biology) include staff management of four people, library operations (library hours, how materials are arranged and displayed, and new services the library will offer), and collections management (selection and de-selection of both monographs and journals). He also spends a lot of time attending library meetings (for good reasons), but he'd like to spend more time working with the faculty. As Parker says, "[Faculty members] are not usually very demanding, but as a result, they are not aware of all the ways the library can help with their teaching, research, and learning; also, the more they know about our services and collections, the more our students will know." With a military background and degrees in English and engineering, Parker is well suited to handle just about any situation that comes his way.

While the main library at UND offers chat reference, gaming nights, Second Life, and wikis (among other tools), Parker and his staff use electronic discussion lists and email but find that what their patrons want most is face-to-face instruction and interaction. The faculty wants "someone to stop by and talk to them, to show a genuine interest in their research and teaching, and to introduce them gently to services that they are not yet using."

Most of the stereotypical comments Parker runs into are related to his gender; he gets a lot of "But guys can't be librarians!" At his previous place of employment, a corporate library, "whenever a colleague and I would work with the consultants, they would usually assume that, because I was the male, I was the supervisor. Since I was the only male in the small library, this annoyed my female boss." Another stereotype he runs into, that seems particular to academia, is when faculty make the assumption that the librarians aren't too bright and therefore should be treated as somewhat humorous servants. "The relationship is not peer to peer, but faculty to staff (regardless of my employment status, which happens to be faculty). Often this is expressed in benign ways, 'You are interested in my research?' (with the implied surprise that I might just understand what that research is). Occasionally it is more obnoxious." Parker's not the only one who's mentioned this particular version of the stereotype; many academic librarians have encountered this type of attitude from their faculty. This is particularly unfortunate, because academic librarians can make the lives of their faculty and staff—through classes, research, and all kinds of efforts—so much easier.

Jenny Levine

Jenny Levine is "not a traditional librarian anymore." She works for the ALA as its Internet Development Specialist and Strategy Guide, an "infamously vague" job title. Jenny, who is in her

early 40s, works to help libraries and librarians—and that's all she does. (All, you say? Ha! Read on.) Her primary responsibilities are to help ALA connect with its members, facilitate interactions between them, and create tools to help implement its initiatives. She is taking ALA to new levels in online interaction with the development of "Online Communities," a robust virtual collaboration workspace; the second phase of development will implement professional networking features. In addition, Jenny teaches and provides technical support to staff members, implements emerging technologies, monitors and maintains 2.0 communication channels, and provides advice and guidance for new initiatives. "All that and the kitchen sink, too."

What Jenny is probably best known for is playing games. Seriously. She's a heavy-duty proponent for learning through gaming in libraries and is helping to lead ALA's gaming initiatives. She recently wrote "Gaming and Libraries: Intersection of Services," an issue of *Library Technology Reports* that addresses what libraries are doing—right here, right now—in terms of gaming. Here, she "illustrate[s] how librarians can reap positive gains by proactively, creatively, and (above all) affordably integrating gaming into the services and programs already offered at your library." Some of the other gaming initiatives from ALA that Jenny handles include a $1 million grant from the Verizon Foundation to explore gaming and literacy in libraries, as well as the ALA TechSource Gaming, Learning, and Libraries Symposium (gaming.tech source.ala.org) and National Gaming in Libraries Day (www.ilovelibraries.org/gaming), both scheduled annually. Like Stephen Abram and Jill Hurst-Wahl, Jenny uses any and every Web 2.0 tool you can think of to connect with her patrons (both ALA members and the public): blogs, RSS, IM, microblogging, social pictures, wikis, podcasts, virtual worlds ... the list goes on and on. You can find Jenny in Twitter, Flickr, Second Life, Facebook, Ning, FriendFeed, and several other socially networked locations.

When asked if she'd ever faced the stereotype, Jenny says,

> I get this all the time, especially the last couple of years since I've been promoting gaming in libraries. When I started my second blog in 2002 [oh, yeah, Jenny's also well-known as The Shifted Librarian; www.theshiftedlibrarian. com], I became known as "the librarian" to readers beyond libraries because there just weren't a lot of other librarians blogging about technology, the changing Internet, and new ways to access information. I would often get comments that these aren't things librarians talk about or that I didn't 'sound like' a librarian. [Maybe it's her training in journalism showing through?] Now with the gaming, people seem continually shocked that a librarian would suggest something that makes noise and doesn't involve books or reading (even though it does, but just in different ways than we're used to thinking about gaming). I've even faced this from within the profession, with a critic implying that I don't care about books and reading,

thereby perpetuating the stereotype that libraries and librarians should only be about books. For me, these kinds of comments mean I'm doing something right since I believe libraries (and librarians) are far more multidimensional than simply being warehouses for print materials with staff sitting behind a desk. Most of the time when someone brings up the stereotype, I just laugh and start listing all of the things libraries (of all types) do that don't focus on books. Usually these turn into great discussions about how libraries have changed since the person was a child and how much we truly offer and serve everyone in the community.

Joseph Murphy

Joseph (Joe) Murphy, an academic librarian in his late 20s, is the General Science Librarian and Instruction Coordinator for the Yale University Science Libraries. This is a long job title, for sure, but what Joe actually does is heavy 21st-century-librarian stuff. Basically, he helps patrons navigate the evolving world of information, and connects them to what they need—face-to-face, virtually, at Yale, while traveling. He's a well-connected librarian! He created and manages an entire social networking setup for Yale Science Libraries (www.library.yale.edu/science/socialnetworking.html); he set up and uses various IM clients and text messaging to provide virtual reference service, employs Twitter to push out updates about the library, and established and manages Facebook, MySpace, and Flickr accounts for the library. His background in physics certainly helps. To add to it all, recently Joe successfully won approval to create and chair the Social Networking subcommittee of the Physics-Astronomy-Mathematics (PAM) division of SLA; over the next year, he'll be showing the division membership how social networking can help PAM.

As with Abigail Goben, Joe's youth has generated a lot of comments, as do his *GQ* looks. "I am half the age of many librarians and I feel that my age has helped to break down several people's stereotypes of librarians. I sometimes even hear that I'm too 'hip' to be a librarian. But I often receive nice responses, like 'wow that's really neat' or 'impressive.' I think that people generally view librarians very positively. As a young male librarian, I encounter a lot of the stereotypes about being a librarian: especially about age, gender, and even sexual orientation. I'm definitely in the minority (which is rare for a straight white male) among librarians in both the common stereotype and real demographics. This forces me to always be very aware of these stereotypes within and beyond libraries." Joe is really gearing up to educate folks about how wrong the stereotype is!

Joshua Neff

Joshua Neff is the Web Content Developer for the Johnson County (KS) Library (JoCo Library; www.jocolibrary.org). He's the go-to guy on the web development team for the JoCoKids (www.jocokids.org) and JoCoTeenScene (www.jocoteenscene.org) sites. (I especially like the various themes available with the click of a mouse on the TeenScene website.) This means designing the webpages, providing blog postings and other content, and working with the children's and teen staff to create new content as well as attending gaming meetings and taking photos for use on the websites. He also regularly blogs for the main library and is working with a school liaison on redesigning the Homework Help pages. The JoCo Library holds frequent gaming events, provides IM reference (through MeeboMe widgets) and RSS feeds on many topics, and has hosted several online author chats through OPAL (Online Programming for All Libraries, www.opal-online.org). Joshua, who is in his late 30s, was also instrumental in creating the Library Society of the World (more on that later).

Starting with an undergraduate degree in English (he worked in the library for most of his undergraduate years), Joshua came to libraries through the Kansas City, Kansas Public Library system. There, he learned that his heart wasn't in teaching English, but in working in libraries. He obtained his Masters in Library and Information Studies from the University of Wisconsin-Milwaukee, returned to Kansas, and has been running around in libraries and library websites ever since. "I like working the reference desk, I like doing web design, I'd like to learn more computer coding, and I love DIY activities, especially in Libraryland." Joshua admitted that he's never really encountered the stereotype, except in the popular media. I was both a bit flabbergasted, and rather pleased!

Kathleen Robertson

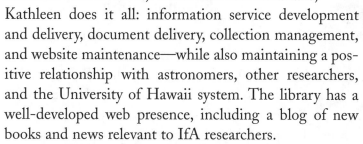

Kathleen Robertson is the Librarian for the Institute for Astronomy (IfA; www.ifa.hawaii.edu/library), part of the University of Hawaii at Manoa. In her early 60s, she is the solo, full-time librarian for IfA, which has facilities on three of the Hawaiian Islands (Oahu, Maui, and the Big Island of Hawaii itself). Like most solo librarians, Kathleen does it all: information service development and delivery, document delivery, collection management, and website maintenance—while also maintaining a positive relationship with astronomers, other researchers, and the University of Hawaii system. The library has a well-developed web presence, including a blog of new books and news relevant to IfA researchers.

Interestingly enough, Kathleen's biggest experience with the librarian stereotype came from other librarians. She says, "When I entered the field of astronomy special libraries in 1990 [after years in archaeology], I was very interested in the handling of observation data. It seemed like the type of data that might benefit from the methods of data field definitions, like MARC, that librarians had developed to handle the huge body of bibliographic information in OCLC, the numeric fields in INSPEC, etc. I asked about any related activities on [a professional] listserv. I was surprised by the hostile responses I received from some colleagues, very much in the 'Librarians don't do that' vein. I was very surprised; it was the first time I'd been 'flamed.' Now with the development of Virtual Observatory projects, I again wonder if some are re-inventing wheels because there is little easy communication between librarians and those tackling the challenges of making vast amounts of data available. In this case, I think that librarians limited themselves by having a too rigid idea of what librarians do and to what they may contribute."

Shannon Smith

Shannon Smith is a young medical solo librarian who left radio news to become a librarian for Uniform Data System for Medical Rehabilitation (www.udsmr.org), a division of University at Buffalo (NY) Foundation Activities. However, her job title is Information Resource Specialist, and her library is called the Information Resource Center. Shannon's primary responsibilities are cataloging and delivery of the collection and reference on request; her duties have expanded from basic searches such as "functional assessment and stroke" to more general "what's new with electronic health records," and include literature reviews and newsletter circulation. She also spends a few hours a week with the IT department. Most of her patron interaction is face-to-face. To quote Shannon, "It's all very satisfying work."

I asked Shannon to share a story about running into the old standby stereotype:

> Given my appearance (I'm in my late 20s, I have tattoos and wear almost entirely punk rock and metal t-shirts outside the office), I don't hold it against anyone who doesn't picture me having any type of career! My husband is a full-time musician, and he's proud to tell people I'm a medical librarian. I play roller derby (as Sheer Tara with the Queen City Roller Girls) and since the league is such a mixed bag of people it is rare someone is fazed to learn what another skater does off the rink; however, outsiders who know me as a derby girl are often shocked or think I'm pulling their leg. One game last year was a spring break/school theme so I co-announced in a costume librarian outfit—PVC skirt, glasses, and all. It was fun to play with the image. The frumpy, shushing librarian stereotype is pervasive but the sexpot in glasses is making its way as an equally ridiculous but more flattering archetype. Being smart is the epitome of sexiness so I don't mind at all when people say straight out that they love hot librarians. Sure, it's a compliment but I welcome it mostly

because it's a step up from people taking "I'm a librarian" to mean I'm a circulation clerk. Apparently many people don't understand that this is a profession.

Librarians and Groups That Break the Stereotype

There are many loud and proud individuals and groups that don't conform to the "typical ideal" for librarians. I'll mention just a few of them; take yourself to your favorite search engine to find more.

Bellydancing Librarians

One of the earliest online groups to celebrate librarians was The Bellydancing Librarian (www.sonic.net/~erisw/bd lib.html). "By day, she toils as a dedicated information professional; by night, she shimmies to the music of the ney, doumbek and oud." Eris Weaver set up the site in the late 1990s because she'd "met so many bellydancing librarians that we could create our own interest group at ALA!" There are a goodly number of librarians featured in the "Gallery of Bellydancing Librarians"; sadly, though, the site hasn't been updated since 2003. (Eris, come back, we need you!) There's also a tribe of belly-dancing librarians on Tribe.net (tribes.tribe.net/belly dancinglibrarians): "This tribe is for librarians, Info

Science people, and anyone who works at a library or in an information field, and who LOVES to bellydance!" The tribe has 61 active members from around the world.

The Butt Kicking Librarians

One group of librarians you don't want to annoy? The Butt Kicking Librarians. Yes, everyone at one time or another refers to themselves as "kicking butt," but this group can actually do it! A group of martial artists from around the U.S. who practice a variety of styles, they collectively fight to keep information freely available to their patrons. The site was started by Andrew Evans (interviewed earlier in this chapter); not only is he the creator of the website, he is chief instructor and owner of Hokkien Martial Arts in Topeka, Kansas, and was recently inducted into the U.S.A. Martial Arts Hall of Fame. To the best of his knowledge, he is the first librarian to be so inducted. (Congratulations, Andrew!) Meet all of the Butt Kicking Librarians at hokkien.uuft.org/librarian.html.

Facebook Librarians

Facebook (www.facebook.com) has really exploded over the past couple of years. Founded in 2004 as a Harvard-only site for incoming freshmen to get to know each other, it took off big-time in the college world and was opened to the general public in 2006. Facebook, needless to say, features about one gazillion groups relating to librarians; some being more professional (there are groups and subgroups for the SLA, ALA, Medical Library Association, Public Library Association, and American Association of Law Libraries, to name just a few) while others are definitely more social. While there are plenty of "Librarians Are Evil" or "I Hate Librarians" sites (most of which appear to be thrown together by disgruntled high schoolers), there are quite a few that touch on the librarian stereotype in one way or another—some with a definite, intentional "anti-stereotype" approach. Here are just a few of the more than 500 groups on Facebook that identify with librarians:

- No, I don't look like a librarian!,
  www.facebook.com/group.php?gid=2251972614

- Yes, I do look like a librarian,
  www.facebook.com/group.php?gid=2272645001

- Do I look like a librarian?,
  www.facebook.com/group.php?gid=2262934453

- I'm a librarian, but I'm not old, I don't own many cats, and work nights,
  www.facebook.com/group.php?gid=2263762244

- Librarians who Twitter,
  www.facebook.com/group.php?gid=5825485883

- Tattooed librarians,
  www.facebook.com/group.php?gid=2431775521

- Librarians with tudes!,
  www.facebook.com/group.php?gid=2228255511

- Sexy librarians,
  www.facebook.com/group.php?&gid=2204977608
  (there are about 10 variations on the title but this is
  the biggest group)

- Second Life librarians,
  www.facebook.com/group.php?&gid=2395106896

- WoW (World of Warcraft) librarians, www.face
  book.com/group.php?&gid=5200354786

The Laughing Librarian

The Laughing Librarian (www.laughinglibrarian.com)
will not be denied! Brian Smith started this collection site
in 1999 and added a blog in 2005. His site is host to a
wide-ranging collection of BibDitties (songs about
libraries from such groups as the anAACRonisms and
Marc Record & the Good Ol' PACs), Koans of the Zen
Librarian (the Zen Librarian said, "Reference service is
like a man hanging from a rope by his teeth over a cliff,
with his hands bound to his sides and feet resting on no
ledge, and another person asks him for books about
Enrico Fermi for a child's school assignment"), a collection of library-related quotes for signature lines, and so
much more. Be sure to check out the Ancient Stories for
Modern Boys section; it's a collection of "contemporary
adaptations of tales that teens will want to read!" My

favorite of the BibDitties is from Lloyd the Library Llama, who sings "The Blogga Song," a hilarious (really—go listen to it right now, I'll wait), sort-of-summary, sort-of-overview, sort-of-introduction to the world of library bloggers that includes a subtle-like-a-big-hammer homage to Blake Carver of LISNews.org. Check them all out at laughinglibrarian.com.

Librarian Avengers

Ah, the Librarian Avenger. Launched in 1997 by a young (and at the time, pre-) librarian and home to the famous "Why you should fall to your knees and worship a librarian" essay, this is one of the good ones. "Want to be a librarian? Got chutzpah? This is the blog for you." Erica Olsen, owner and proprietor of the site, is both a librarian and a programmer; she blogs about interesting cross-sections of the two, beekeeping, Second Life, cats, and misuse of punctuation, among other things. By far, though, her site is known for the "Worship" essay—I've seen it on doors (it's center stage on mine!) and bulletin boards and linked from websites, by folks who aren't sure who put it together but think it's a perfect example of what we do. "Many people think of librarians as diminutive civil servants, scuttling about 'Sssh-ing' people and stamping things. Well, think again buster." Yes! Go forth and worship at librarianavengers.org.

Library Society of the World

By far the group with the most current potential is the Library Society of the World (LSW). The LSW is "a world-spanning group of library professionals and library advocates, dedicated to furthering the role of librarians, archivists, information professionals, and information educators through communication and collaboration. The LSW is about people, not buildings (although some of us think architecture is sexy). It's about friendship, not organization. It's about creating and fostering opportunities, not building barriers and divisions." Started by librarian Joshua Neff (featured earlier in this chapter) in April 2007, in the short time it's been around the LSW has collected a large, diverse, and international membership that continues to expand. Regular LSW meetups are starting to happen at all the major library conferences, and LSW has become a central clearinghouse for library "unconferences" as well. (An unconference is an in-person, participant-driven conference centered on a theme or purpose that lacks big fees, speakers, and idea tracks; basically, the participants decide the path of the conference as it goes.) The idea of the LSW has been embraced by more than just librarians; at the 2008 ALA Annual Conference, science fiction author and blogger Cory Doctorow sported an LSW badge ribbon (tinyurl.com/5qmtx4)! Read more, or join up, at librarysociety.pbwiki.com or at the newly created thelsw.org.

Library Underground

Another bastion of hipness and grooviness is the Library Underground, "a guide to alternative library culture on the world wide web." The Library Underground comprises another wide range of librarians, with some overlap with the other groups listed here. It contains links to sites on activism, sexuality, weirdness, fun and games (including a link to a game where you can rearrange Melvil Dewey's face), news sources, and even librarian-run web stores. The group has an associated list that can be counted on to provide random insights into politics, strange reference questions, and upcoming librarian gatherings. Join the underground at www.libraryunder ground.org.

The Lipstick Librarian

Any list of librarians who poke fun at the stereotype would be incomplete without mention of the Lipstick Librarian. Created in 1997 by Linda Absher, this is a site for everyone who needs a bit of humor injected into the profession. "She's Bold! She's Sassy! She's Helpful! She's … a Lipstick Librarian!" Linda also blogs about the Days and Nights of the Lipstick Librarian, talking about ALA, politics, pop culture, music, shoes, Hurricane Katrina, and, oh, everything else. I rarely get through a blog posting without at least a chuckle; sometimes I laugh out loud, and it's so hard to explain why to co-workers. Put this one on your "must read" blog list, at lipstick librarian.com.

The Modified Librarian

Another of the oldest (yet defunct—it hasn't been updated since 1999) sites celebrating the nontraditional librarian is the Modified Librarian. The site was intended to "discuss the concept and practice of body modification as it relates to librarians as persons and professionals" and included a gallery of tattooed and pierced librarians, as well as "rants" from same. This is the spiritual forerunner of the "Tattooed Librarians" group on Facebook, and I still get questions related to the site. (This is another site, like the original Bellydancing Librarian, that I'd love to see resurrected.) The idea of tattooed librarians as an eyebrow-raiser in popular culture was tempting enough for Archie McPhee (of Librarian Action Figure fame) to bring out a set of "The Illustrated Librarian Temporary Tattoos," featuring such designs as a winged book with a banner below saying "Read or Die," and a heart shape with glasses and a banner reading "Librarians Rule" (www.mcphee.com/items/11696.html). It's almost gotten to the point where mentions of bodyart are incidental to librarianship—and that's just the way it should be. View the Modified Librarian at www.bmeworld.com/gailcat.

Radical Reference Librarians

If you're looking for "answers for those who question authority," I suggest you look no further than the Radical Reference Librarians. Started in 2004 to provide street-level instant advice to demonstrators at that year's

Republican National Convention in New York City, it has evolved into a multilingual site (primarily English and Spanish, with volunteers available in seven other languages) to "answer questions from activists and independent journalists on topics related to those activities." Radical Reference is staffed by volunteer librarians from across the planet and is dedicated to information activism. If you really want insight into Radical Reference, be sure to check out the list of questions they've answered (all questioners remain anonymous); these range from finding documentation about uprisings at women's prisons and the number of people in immigrant detention in the years since 9/11 to community gardening resources and how book sales are broken down. This is a fascinating look into reference librarianship, at radicalreference.info.

The Warrior Librarian

All hail Biblia the Warrior Librarian! (Or else …) Thanks to Amanda Credaro and her wicked sense of humor, the library world can enjoy 255 wonderful issues of the Warrior Librarian Weekly newsletter, calling attention to librarianship issues, both silly and serious, from around the world. The best part of the site, however, has to be the amazing collection of humor items, all written by Amanda. She even has a book published with a collection of her writings, some from the website but most created specifically for *Biblia's Guide to Warrior Librarianship*, subtitled "Humor for

Librarians who Refuse to be Classified." Two of the most popular pages to date include Collective Nouns for Librarians and OPAC Error Messages; there are many more, and I highly recommend you check out the site at warriorlibrarian.com.

Thoughts on the Future

Fortunately, a small segment of our population, librarians, has been dealing with the problem of information organization since 2000 B.C. Who better to turn to in our time of need than people with thousands of years of accumulated expertise and experience?

—Eugene Eric Kim

We've looked at the classic stereotype of librarians; we've looked at current media representations of librarians; and we've met modern librarians who are anything but the stereotype and who are defining a new image of librarians. But what about the future? Where are we, as a profession, heading? How will users' perceptions change along with our changing roles? And what can we do—right here, right now—to make that journey fulfilling? We all agree on one thing: Everything is changing. The image, the perception, the skills, the job itself—*everything.*

Science fiction presents us with possible future truths, and many science fiction writers are also scientists and futurists. Isaac Asimov was all three, and, in his Foundation series, he wrote librarians right into the essential fabric of the future universe. In the Foundation's *Encyclopaedia Galactica* (www.orionsarm.com/eg/l/Li-Ln.html#librarian), he wrote: "In the info-flood that is the modern galaxy, librarians are an essential group that is necessary for everyday functioning in the worlds of the nexus." Asimov's words from the 1950s tidily sum up the world we live in now. Flooded by information and continually connected through the nexus of the Internet, we are beginning to see more organizations turn to (and back to) librarians to help sort through the glut—to help them function in the information age. But we're not there yet; much work remains to be done.

Changing Roles

The traditional role of librarian as middleman between information and end users is going away and is being replaced by that of librarian as information guide and facilitator. As Seth Godin (www.sethgodin.com), author, change agent, marketing guru, and Squidoo founder, said in his Special Libraries Association (SLA) 2008 keynote, "Gatekeepers are out. Personal dissemination is in." American Library Association past president Sarah Long expands on this in a 2005 column, saying that, "Today the critical need for librarians is to serve as interpreters and guides to the vast array of information that exists." This is so true! Those same people who used to say "Why do we need librarians, anyway, if everything is on the Internet?" are starting to realize that "everything" is an awful lot. They are coming back to us to ask for help in sorting out the relevant and important bits of information from the firehose flood.

As Abigail Goben (see Chapter 3) says, "just because there is a glut of information out there doesn't mean our society has been magically endowed with the ability to navigate and understand it all." In the legal world, law firms that closed in-house libraries because they weren't "bringing in revenue" are now re-opening them—because they've realized that having a professional law librarian on hand actually saves them time and money. In the science world, observatories that haven't had librarians, or once had one and then redefined the position, are now looking for someone to help them re-organize their archives and data. This change in perspective is taking place gradually but inexorably.

Academic and research libraries will likely change most dramatically over the foreseeable future. They are facing an "age of transformation," confronting the need to reevaluate and re-create their plans for interacting with students and faculty. The Association of College and Research Libraries (ACRL) produced a 2007 report titled "Changing Roles of Academic and Research Libraries" that discusses and analyzes these coming changes in detail. One line stands out: "The changes that are occurring—in technology, in research, teaching and learning—have created a very different context for the missions of academic and research libraries. This evolving context can afford a moment of opportunity if libraries and librarians can respond to change in proactive and visionary ways." If this response is successful—and it will have to be, as incoming students and new researchers are likely to be technologically immersed—it could elevate the importance of libraries on campus to a whole new level. Collaboration will also evolve to new heights, not just between librarians and their patrons but between librarians in different areas of the same library. Create Change (www.createchange.org), a website developed by the Association of Research Libraries for academic research, asks "Shouldn't the way we share research be as advanced as the Internet?" The site sets about exploring ways to change the way we work.

Law and other special libraries will also change, along with their librarians' roles. In March 2008, Aspatore Books published *The Changing Role of Law Firm Librarianship*. This work discusses "major elements of the librarian's role today, including new marketing responsibilities, coordination with information technology departments, and the expanding presence of the library within the firm." A collection of essays from legal librarians all over the country, it echoes the statements I often hear from law librarians, discussing the changing information landscape, how to use emerging technologies most efficiently, and balancing budgets to get the most from funding.

Every type of library, and every librarian, faces similar issues. Mila Ramos, Chief Librarian of the International Rice Research Institute, presented a paper in 2007 for the 35th Agricultural Librarians Association of the

Philippines meeting titled "The Role of Librarians in the 21st Century," and she mentioned the same changes in the information landscape and the need to effectively incorporate emerging technologies. She lists some core competencies needed by librarians in the digital age: "knowledge in the areas of information resources, information access, technology management, and research plus the ability to apply them in providing library and information services." Even public librarians are seeing this shift; folks don't just ask for help finding an almanac anymore but help with formatting Office documents or setting up an email account.

Our power has always been in our ability to guide others in how to find the information they seek; that power still exists and is still needed.

Changing Skill Sets

We're also going to see a significant change in skill sets. Library schools are starting to teach more about information technology—as well they should; the days when library and information technology tasks were separate have long gone. Those librarians who have dismissed technology simply will not be able to do so anymore; librarians must embrace becoming technologically proficient. As with any profession, some members are on the forefront of adopting, and adapting, new technologies and tools for use in libraries. But, our profession as a whole will move more toward implementing newer technologies, instead of just those few currently out front.

Each major library association and specialized subfield provides a list of basic, core competencies, along with more extensive lists of professional and personal competencies, that librarians should be aware of and do their best to keep up with. The basic core skill set for all librarians, however, is heading in the same direction: We need to accept that new technologies are going to be a part of our library lives and embrace change. This change should also increase our visibility; as Stephen Abram has said, "We need to identify ourselves as professionals; we need to drop the humility and anonymity issues and get ourselves out there." Antony Brewerton phrases it best: "As a profession, we need to give out the message—in any medium available—that we are not the refuge of the quiet and scared, that we are not living in the 19th Century, but that this is a confident, go ahead, passionate profession with its heart on its sleeve rather than its hair in a bun." Laura Carscaddon succinctly says, "Speak up or die out." That may be difficult for those of us more used to working in the background, but we need to get over it and put ourselves out there.

As I mentioned, our power has always been—and continues to be—in our ability to guide others to find the information they seek. We're all familiar with the flood of information inundating today's users, and we know that we can help. Change is hard, but think about how this change in roles can revitalize, challenge, inspire, and stimulate us. Isn't it a kick to help a patron discover exactly what it was they were looking for? Or when you and your team finally get a grasp on your new website design? Or when a student thanks you? We all face a changing information landscape; it's up to us to invite and allow that change into our own experience.

Virtual Worlds

Speaking of adopting and adapting new technologies, many librarians feel we are heading toward an entirely new way to interact: virtual worlds. Many librarians now use virtual communication techniques to interact with their patrons—text and instant messaging, for example— and others are beginning to branch out into full multi-user virtual environments (MUVEs).

Jambina Oh, Amy Buckland's Second Life alter-ego,
listening to a talk in-world at McGill University Library Island

Eighty percent of Internet users are expected to engage in some form of virtual world activity by 2011, according to the Gartner Research Group (www.gartner.com). While there are many MUVEs out there, most of them focus on gaming/adventure, such as World of Warcraft or Age of Conan.

At this time, Second Life (SL; secondlife.com) is the most used nongaming virtual world. A free world created by Linden Lab and released in 2003, SL is a "3-D virtual world created by its Residents"—and as of August 2008, it had 14.8 *million* users. Not only can you build a version of yourself for use in-world, called an avatar, but you can also buy and sell land and property using Linden dollars, which have a real-world monetary equivalent. Many universities, organizations, and corporations have invested time and money in SL; as noted in Chapter 3, some librarians dedicate a substantial portion of their time to building tools and providing reference services in-world. University classes are held in-world, with all interactions, lectures, instructor office hours, and study groups being done online. It's a whole new take on distance education! Illinois' Alliance Library System (www.alliancelibrarysystem.com) and OPAL (Online Programming for All Libraries) have collaborated to create Info Island (infoisland.org) and the Alliance Virtual Library, which provides education courses, reference services, book discussion groups, GLBT centers, art galleries, performances, and more. Cybrary City, associated with Info Island, is home to many academic and public libraries; in addition to real-world events in the brick-and-mortar library buildings, several public libraries are

*Jill Hurst-Wahl's avatar, Jillianna Suisei, in front of the
SLA space under construction in Second Life*

now offering in-world events such as author talks and storytelling events.

How do these interactions in virtual worlds affect people's perceptions of librarians? Well, for starters, librarians tend to choose decidedly nonstereotypical avatars—which is unsurprising if you realize that librarians do come in all shapes, sizes, and colors, but can be startling to people who still think of us as Marian the Librarian. Our in-world interactions also provide a fabulous opportunity for us to show folks that, yes, librarians *do* do things, like this, that buck popular perceptions. Librarian participation in virtual worlds also helps people—especially the increasingly wired newer generations—understand that we will continue to be there for them, wherever they need us. For example: Let's say that a student is researching IBM, in part through IBM's many SL presences. When that student finds that she can get reference help from a librarian right there, within SL—rather than having to leave SL, find a librarian, and ask—it changes her view of librarians and increases use of in-world reference services. This also, in turn, gives in-world librarians an advantage when later dealing with students in real life.

This all can be cool and groovy, but we must also remember that not everyone is online. We've all heard of the "digital divide." If we move to a purely virtual world of information exchange, what does that do to the have-nots in this equation? We also cannot assume that even connected folks know what they're doing; just because they have a computer doesn't mean they know how to use it properly, let alone how to navigate through the data flood to the information they actually need. We—librarians and our libraries—will have a much greater role to play in bridging this digital divide. We're seeing it already: classes in basic computer use, classes in using search engines, classes in how to use word processing software. These folks are not ready for SL just yet, and we can help them move toward the goal of computer proficiency. This will be most important in rural areas, where according to the Pew Internet & American Life (www.pewinternet.org) research group's August 2008 demographics of U.S. Internet users, almost 25 percent of folks are not online (www.pewinternet.org/trends/User_Demo_10%2020%2008.htm). We also need to be aware that not everyone has access to high-speed transfer rates;

Pew numbers also show that broadband Internet in American homes has increased 8 percent between 2007 and 2008, but it's still only at 55 percent of the population, and primarily in higher-income homes (www.pew internet.org/PPF/r/257/report_display.asp). There's that digital divide again! Why is this so important? In the words of Pew's John Horrigan, "The fuss about broadband extends beyond access to information to active participation in the online commons as people with shared interests or problems gather at various online forums to chat or collaborate" (www.pewinternet.org/PPF/r/224/report_display.asp).

One unfortunate component of the sterotypical view of librarians is that of technological shyness or incompetence. Everyone, sooner or later, will need access to these online common spaces as more and more companies and organizations move in that direction. When we are able to help people participate in these new online areas, it can be a great way to combat that outdated view.

Community Spaces

That's a nice segue to another topic many librarians agree on: Libraries will become community spaces again, places where the ideas of commons and community return. Regardless of how closely your local librarian resembles Marian the Librarian, librarians have always been an integral part of these community spaces. Dictionary.com defines commons as "pertaining or belonging equally to an entire community, nation, or culture; public." Community

is defined as "a group of people having common interests." Dr. Ann Curry explains in the material for her
graduate course on Planning and Designing Libraries
that "libraries have a long tradition of providing interior
public space, with the public library as the foremost
example of a place offering unfettered access to all.
Although traditional and modern functions of a library
are paramount design considerations, the role the library
plays to provide public space cannot be ignored if the
library is to fulfill its mandate to serve" (tinyurl.com/
5clpgv). The roles librarians play in this service mandate
also cannot be ignored. It takes the participation and
interaction of librarians with their patrons to make it
happen, and we're going to see that function grow and
expand in the future.

Commons does not just refer to the "Information
Commons" that are part and parcel of most universities
these days, but to the role of public libraries as well.
Richard Akerman says it well in a blog posting from July
22, 2008 (tinyurl.com/5afnrq) titled "the public library is
for: the public," where he discusses the need for a new
Ottawa Public Library:

- The city is for its citizens.

- The public library is for the public.

- Public space is essential to a healthy urban
  environment.

- The central public library provides one of the few remaining opportunities to enhance and enlarge public space.

He then goes on to discuss how a vibrant city provides places for its citizens to "meet and think and be." This is echoed by the Project for Public Spaces (PPS), which says in a newsletter article titled "How to Make Your Library Great" that "when everything works together, libraries become places that anchor community life and bring people together" (www.pps.org/info/newsletter/april2007). PPS is working together with Libraries for the Future (www.lff.org) and the Americans for Libraries Council to help public libraries across the nation transform themselves into "21st century community centers for information and education." I really recommend a read of their entire newsletter from April 2007; this alone discusses 14 lessons that a great library should learn, such as fostering communication, providing easy access, and supporting functions, and then gives point-by-point examples of libraries around the country doing just that. The feature story of the newsletter is "Why Libraries Matter More than Ever"—and we can all agree! "The creation of the 'information superhighway' threatened to make libraries obsolete, but today they are as prominent as ever. Libraries are taking on a larger civic role, redefining themselves as community centers for the 21st Century." Also in the issue are examples of Library Placemaking in Action and an article on creating a great civic space.

One way we can close the participation gap as part of this community mandate is to include patrons in what we do—they are part of our community, after all. In some libraries, patrons are not only allowed but encouraged to contribute to the library's public wiki, leave notes and recommendations in the catalog, or contribute to reader's advisory lists. The East Lansing (MI) Public Library (www.elpl.org), has an online patron review site where patrons answer the question: "Do you have a favorite book, movie, or album that you can't stop raving about? Or perhaps you've just finished the worst book ever and want to warn others?" Among other systems, the Butler University (IN) Libraries' Reference Wiki (www.seed wiki. com/wiki/butler_wikiref) is open to staff and students alike for contributions. Many libraries have implemented video contests for patrons using YouTube. The Hennepin County Library in Minnesota offers BookSpace (www.hc lib.org/pub/bookspace), an online reading community where you not only get advice on books to read, but can post your own reviews.

And, what about a social library catalog, where patrons are encouraged to add notes and recommendations directly to the card catalog? It's been talked about rather explosively and actually implemented by the Biblio Commons (bibliocommons.com) package (which can be installed over an existing ILS), and rolled out for real-life use in July 2008 at the Oakville Public Library in Ontario, Canada (www.opl.on.ca). Another real-life implementation is SOPAC 2.0, a social catalog system built by John Blyberg, the Head of Technology and Digital Initiatives at the Darien (CT) Library (www.darienlibrary.org). Blyberg rolled out version 1.0 during his tenure at the Ann Arbor (MI) District Library (www.aadl.org/catalog), but this prototype was, as he says, a collection of hacks. He has since moved to the Darien Library, and he and his team have completely rebuilt SOPAC as a solid software product usable with just about any library system—which they're releasing as open source software. This is a huge, extremely innovative, and forward-thinking step in the world of social networking and libraries; by releasing it as open source, Blyberg and the team at Darien are making it easy for other libraries to take the same step. Read more on SOPAC 2.0 at Blyberg's own blog (www.blyberg.net/2008/08/16/sopac-20-what-to-expect).

These tools all help contribute to the library as a common space; hand-in-hand with the sharing capabilities these tools can provide, the path toward the new library will broaden, emphasizing even more the connectedness between users (staff, patrons, even international collaboration). Michael Stephens, of Dominican University and the Tame the Web blog (www.tametheweb.com), teaches his students that "the future of libraries will be guided by how users access, consume, and create content. Content is a conversation as well, and librarians should participate. Users will create their own mash ups, remixes, and original expressions and should be able to do so at the library or via the library's resources." Vint Cerf, speaking at the 2008 SLA Annual Conference, alluded to the same thing when he said "the most exciting vision that I have is that somehow when this is mature we will—every one of us—have access to all of the information that every one of us wants to share." And as we, librarians and our libraries, progress toward this evolutionary goal, "libraries can help return the national conversation to a civil discourse, creating a space where diverse groups can come together," suggests Jenny Levine.

Now What?

What now? We can see that "everyone" is right—things *are* changing, in many ways. Librarians are more necessary in the digital age than ever before, and organizations (as the Elsevier and LexisNexis ads indicate) are beginning to recognize that librarians do belong on the team. Amy Buckland sums it up by noting that "it will become normal to have a librarian in your Rolodex." And yet, according to my summer 2008 survey, we're still seeing the persistence of the old stereotype—which includes the belief that librarians *can't* do it; we just can't handle social changes and technological advances.

To combat the stereotypes, we need to step up what we're already doing. In our day-to-day activities, we need to show our patrons (and anyone else we meet) what we're capable of. When someone expresses surprise, or says "I didn't know librarians did that!" explain that yes, indeed, we do, and a lot more besides. Make a point of attending career days at local schools or local organizations, and share your passion for what you do. In early 2008 I participated in a "Women in Science and Education" career workshop (ws.web.arizona. edu/wise)—and heard a roomful of teenage girls tell me that they didn't realize librarians could do what I do.

This, though, is just the first step. What else can we do to change the stereotype? Most importantly: Don't be afraid of change. Don't be afraid of technology. Don't be afraid if your role changes to become more collaborative with your patrons (come out from behind the desk!). Don't be afraid of your IT department—many would love to work with you to make your experience—and that of your users—better. Don't be afraid to try something technologically new or to play with a new tool; you never know what you might find and how it might benefit you.

Embrace new learning: Check into continuing education courses at your local college or the professional development courses offered by national associations. You may be surprised to find a new way of thinking about your day-to-day activities or by new insight into your users' needs. Accept new modes of interaction; even if you don't dive into SL or another MUVE, be aware that they exist and are being used as powerful learning and educational tools. Lastly, start using social networking tools if you haven't yet; the social web truly is the world of the future, and the sooner you get hooked into that world, the better.

Academic librarians should learn about blended librarianship (www.blendedlibrarian.org), or the integration of the library into the teaching and learning process. Many academic librarians are working closely and successfully with professors and schools in their academic areas of responsibility. Yes, you'll hear horror stories about how bad these relationships can get—but there are good examples, too, just as with IT departments, and it's worth it to try and make things work. Public librarians should be ready to get out there with their patrons. Help make your community space a true part of the community. Sometimes this means thinking outside the box—and sometimes it means working completely outside the library. But, you are the key to your library being a community space. Special librarians should make the effort to integrate themselves into their user base. Your users may benefit from amazing tools from areas outside your expertise. Find them, become familiar with them, and then make your users aware of them; not only will you expand your skill set, but you'll show exactly why you're an important part of the team. All librarians should be ready to laugh off, "But librarians don't do that!" Back it up with what we do best—provide information!

If you aren't a librarian, thank you for reading this book. I hope this experience has helped show you that librarians are pretty awesome! If you are a librarian, thank you for reading this book. If you take one message away from all of this, above all, be "loud and proud" about being a librarian, whether you have the word "librarian" in your job title or not. Speak up! Step out! Stay out there, or get out there, to educate, inform, and assist!

You Don't Look Like a Librarian: Librarians' Views of Public Perception in the Internet Age

This appendix will summarize some of the results from the original "You Don't Look Like a Librarian" survey, conducted in 2001 and reported on at the 2002 Annual Special Libraries Association meeting. (You can find the complete version, including the 2001 data, on the "You Don't Look Like a Librarian" website at www.librarian-image.net/perc.html). A second identical survey was performed in 2008 for comparison purposes over time. The survey was originally prompted by the number of comments I received about not "looking like a librarian"—the same impetus as the website, articles, columns, and even this book. You could say this is what started this entire ball rolling!

Survey and Methodology

The survey of librarians was originally sent out in December 2001 to several library-focused email discussion lists; the same questions were reposted on email discussion lists, Twitter, and my blog in the summer of 2008. In hindsight, some of the questions should have been phrased more clearly; because I wanted a direct comparison, though, I didn't change the wording between the two surveys. The survey questions were:

- What's your gender?

- What's your age range?

- Where are you located? (state/country)

- Do you have a college degree(s)? If so, in what?

- What year did you graduate? Or, how many years have you spent in librarianship?

- What type of library do you work in?

- What's your title? Has your title changed recently, and if so, to what?

- What's your salary range?

- What are your hobbies/activities outside work?

- Do fellow hobbyists comment on your profession? Are comments generally more positive or negative?

- Do you get other comments, in general, about your appearance related to your job? (Too young, too old, "I didn't know librarians dressed like that!" etc.?)

- Do you feel that the public perception of librarians has changed in the last 10 years? For better or worse?

- Do you have a favorite recent (since 1990) portrayal of librarians in media (books, movies, etc.)? Or, do you have a recent portrayal that you really dislike?

- Do you have any short stories you'd like to share that have happened to you in relation to your appearance and profession?

As you can see, these questions strike a balance between statistical happiness and social reporting. From the first survey (2001), I received 337 responses; to the second survey (2008), which was advertised via email discussion lists and also on my blog and my Twitter feed, I received 1,215. Let's take a look at the statistical results, reported as percentages to ease comparison.

Survey Results

Unsurprisingly, both times most of my survey respondents were women, but the balance is oh-so-slightly shifted in the latter survey. And male librarians still get hit with the usual, "But guys can't be librarians" line—a lot of respondents mentioned it.

What's your gender?

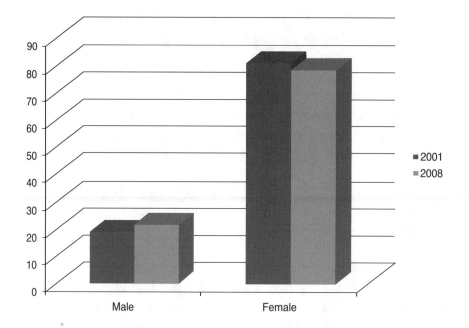

The ages of survey respondents didn't hold many surprises, either; the distribution is slightly different, with the peak for 2001 occurring in the 40s and the peak in 2008 occurring in the 30s. What this means for the "graying of the profession" issue, I don't know. Considering, though, that some 2008 respondents were actively working in libraries into their 70s, I'd say there's some graying (as with every profession), but they aren't going anywhere!

What's your age range?

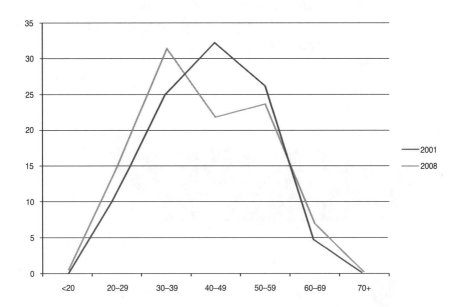

Location—well, that was a pleasant discovery! In the first survey, I heard from 31 international respondents, and in the second from 170; but where those respondents answered from has widened dramatically. In 2001, I got responses from all over the U.S. and from Argentina, Canada, Croatia, the Netherlands, New Zealand, South Africa, Sweden, and Switzerland. Things have definitely gone more international in the intervening years; in the 2008 survey, I heard from 37 countries in addition to the U.S.: Argentina, Australia, Brazil, Canada, Chile, China, Croatia, Denmark, Egypt, Ethiopia, the European Union, France, Germany, Hong Kong, India, Indonesia, Ireland, Israel, Italy, Malta, Morocco, Namibia, New

Caledonia, New Zealand, Norway, Philippines, Scotland, South Africa, South Korea, Spain, Sri Lanka, Sweden, Switzerland, Turkey, United Kingdom, Virgin Islands, and Zimbabwe.

Where are you located?

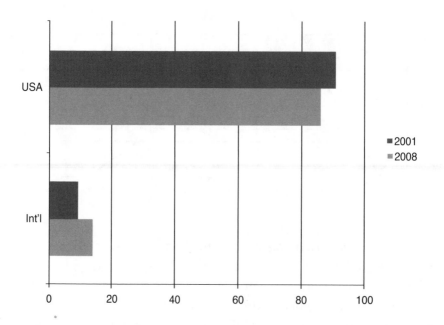

It's always interesting to see how we all came into librarianship. In addition to various degrees in librarianship, respondents held degrees in:

- Anthropology

- Astrophysics

- Biochemistry

- Broadcasting

- Chemical Engineering

- Counseling

- Dance History and Choreography

- Entomology

- Fashion Design

- Forest Biology

- Government Studies

- Horticulture

- International Affairs

- Justice Studies

- Law

- Linguistics

- Marine Biology

- Molecular Biology

- Neuroscience

- Paleontology

- Psychobiology

- Russian/Eastern European Studies

- Scandinavian Studies

- Speech Pathology

- Theology

- Wildlife Biology

- Women's Studies

- Zoology

The amount of time folks have spent working in libraries also wasn't entirely surprising; the percentages show a high number of relative newcomers, with a steady decrease after that point. Again, compared to the 2001 numbers, in 2008 there were more responses from folks who'd been actively working in libraries for more than 40 years; similar to the age ranges, this shows that the profession may be graying but it's also keeping that knowledge and wisdom around.

Do you have a college degree(s)?

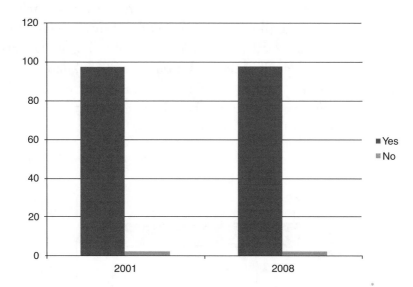

How many years have you spent in librarianship?

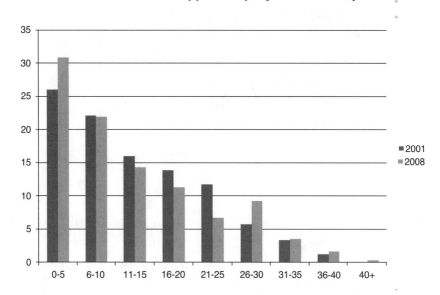

The type of library reported by respondents saw quite a change over the past seven years. I wasn't entirely surprised that the 2001 survey returned such a high number from corporate, private, or other libraries, as the survey had originally been sent around to special, law, and solo librarians, most of which fell into that category. The numbers from 2008 should more accurately reflect the spread of library types.

What type of library do you work in?

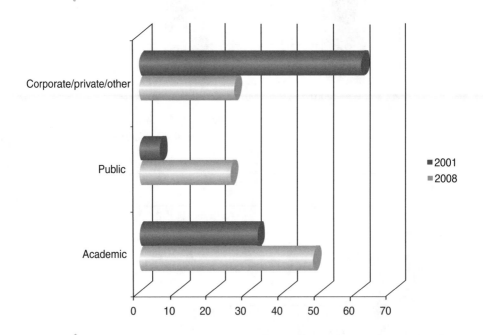

This is where things started to get interesting. We all know (see Chapter 1) that we quite often work in a job where we're called something other than Librarian. This title change has been happening over the last decade or so, as more and more libraries and corporations move toward embracing the idea of information science. But, the numbers that came back from the survey really brought home how much it's changed! The widespread difference in titles that librarians went by in 2001 is no longer so widespread.

What's your title?

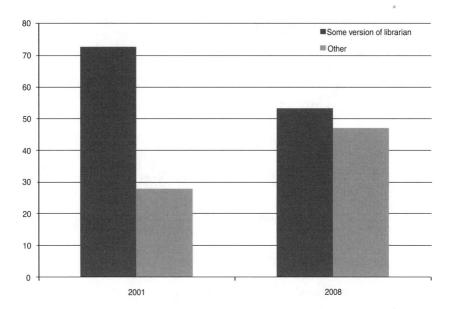

The variation in the titles that librarians go by these days, other than some version of Librarian, is also astonishing. In 2001, the most popular nonlibrarian job title was Information Specialist. In 2008, there was no clear frontrunner (Information Specialist only appeared 15 times). Today, these titles include:

- Analyst

- Archivist

- Bibliographic Data Manager

- Business Systems Analyst

- Competitive Intelligence Analyst

- Data Bank Coordinator

- Digital Reference Specialist

- Director of Strategic Programs

- Documentalist

- Independent Information Specialist

- Information Architect

- Information Specialist

- Knowledge Manager

- Materials Selector

- Network Administrator

- Open Source Evangelist

- Principal Information Specialist

- Public Services Coordinator

- Standards and Guidance Coordinator

- Systems Administrator

- Technical Resource Analyst

- Technology Coordinator

- Virtual Branch Administrator

- Virtual Library Manager

- Web Designer

- Web Information Specialist

It's quite an array, isn't it?

Money. Well, this is always an issue. As you can see in the related graph, the data from the two surveys have the same shape, but after the peak numbers in the $40–$49K range, the 2008 numbers take over (which means more people are making higher salaries in 2008 than in 2001).

I enjoy sharing my profession with casual inquirers, and always make a point of doing so when I'm at a social gathering. Not everyone does, as the responses from both surveys show; quite a few folks said they had "solo hobbies" or "didn't interact with others." But, among those who did interact with others, almost three-quarters of them heard comments of one type or another.

What's your salary range? (in USD)

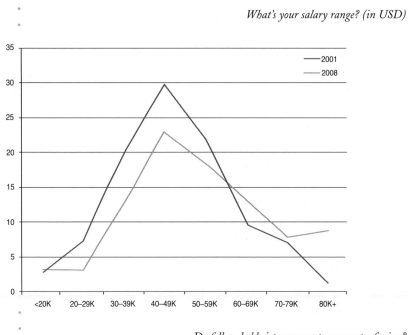

Do fellow hobbyists comment on your profession?

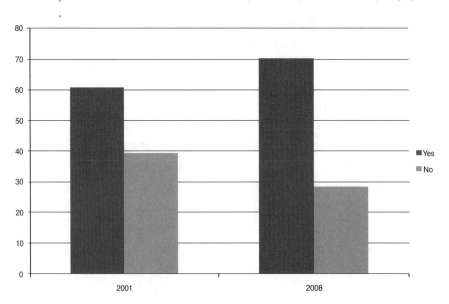

Are comments generally more positive or negative?

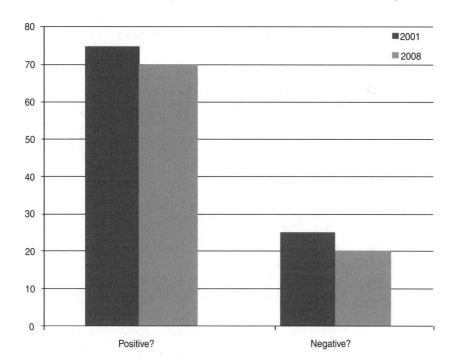

Some of the comments are telling, not just from fellow hobbyists but from people in general, as the following quotes from the 2008 survey respondents demonstrate:

- "Mostly, people are surprised about library science being an actual career, and something you can study in college."

- "Wahoo! You studied 3 years to learn the alphabet? Great!"

- "They're just confused, and don't understand it."

- "Positive, though I think most people have the impression that I sit at a desk all day, checking out books. They don't understand what librarians actually *do*."

- "Yes—mostly positive, usually followed by a request for help or advice. Academic faculty sometimes make slightly negative comments based on their perception that librarianship is not as intellectually rigorous as their own work."

- "Believe it's easy, no stress, get to read books all day, have no idea it requires a master's degree."

- "They crack jokes … I don't think they are trying to be negative, but they are."

- "I have gotten the 'You're a Librarian??' from some of the kids, but I think it's mostly because they can't believe a Librarian knows more about *Battlestar Galactica* than they do."

- "You don't *sound* like a librarian—I thought librarians were quiet."

- "Surprise at my age ('You're older than my mom!' in shocked tones). 'You don't look like a librarian!' (clothing and/or hair); people are especially surprised if they see me carrying swords (for dancing)—doesn't seem to fit with their idea of what a librarian does!"

- "You don't look like one of them."

- "You're the head of the Library!?!?!? I thought you were one of the shelvers."

- "Silent, semi-stunned looks of disbelief."

- "I get '*You're* a librarian' all the time. I guess it comes from the generally fashionable clothes, hair-cut, and ability to converse about pop culture ..."

- "I get comments like 'You wore that to work?' (I wear a lot of spangles) and when I tell them I'm a librarian they say 'Oh, well then.' Librarians, I guess, get to wear anything they want."

- "If I knew librarians dressed like that I'd go to the library more often."

- "Jokes about where are my sensible shoes and cardigan. Jokes when I do happen to look like the stereotype because my hair is up. Generally that I don't look like one for various reasons."

- "One time someone asked me why I had a 'women's' job."

- "People are surprised to find a white, male, Republican working in a library."

- "*You're* a librarian?! But you look so normal!"

- "I didn't know you were a librarian, I thought you were faculty."

- "You're the librarian? Well you can't be old enough to have completed a degree."

- "Are you a librarian? You look too young to be able to answer my question."

- "I get both sides. From older patrons I get 'You don't look like a librarian' and from my peers I get, 'you look exactly like a librarian.'"

- "Only a surprised look, or the odd 'so you must be gay.'"

- "Many people seem to find male librarians suspect."

- "Invariably, someone will comment on not having my hair in a bun or glasses on the tip of my nose. There's always some reference to shushing people all day."

And now, for the big question: Do you (librarians) think the perception of librarians has changed over the last 10 to 15 years? I did hope that the last seven years would result in a higher percentage of people answering yes; sadly, though, that was not the case.

A large number of the "yes" answers were qualified with "a little bit" or "slightly." Many people answered that

Do you feel that the public perception of librarians has changed?

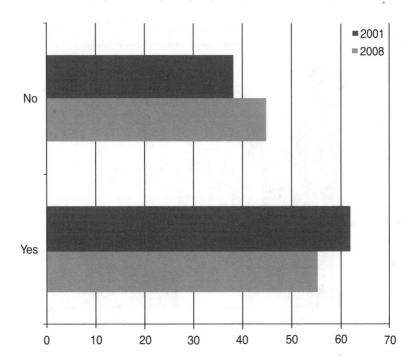

they felt the idea of librarians had changed, but for the worse. Their comments include:

- "Still the stereotype of the old lady with glasses, or the 'hot' librarian who takes down her hair and whips off her glasses."

- "Not enough—nonlibrarians still think we're all about shushing and shelving; it's infuriating."

- "Worse: underpaid and underappreciated for the work we do."

Has perception changed for the better?

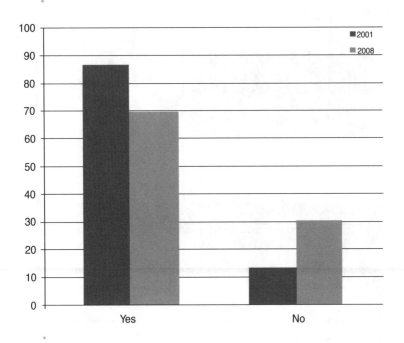

- "It really depends who you ask. Because of the strong response to the PATRIOT Act, I know a number of people who have said they were impressed by librarians taking on that issue. Others, however, view the same thing negatively. For the most part, though, people still don't seem to have a clue what the job actually entails. Most people think I just 'check out books.'"

- "For the better, mostly we are ignored or taken for granted, and in today's public schools you want to be ignored ..."

- "Worse; people are more independent on computers, less library-bound, and in general, there's a perception that the profession has remained in the past for particularly public, somewhat academic, and even slightly corporate librarianship."

- "For better, but it's very slow and limited to certain areas."

- "For the better publicly, for the worse in academia of all sorts."

- "Marginal movement."

- "Probably for the better. I think we're probably seen as less stodgy, though maybe now some conservatives see us more as elitist, left-wing radicals."

- "Generally better except for those who ask why libraries are still needed since we have the Internet."

- "Worse—we're increasingly seen as irrelevant."

- "Only marginally, in some cases for better as in librarians do all the behind the scenes web stuff and for worse as in who needs you anymore."

It's hard to say whether the answers I've gotten from these library surveys are good or bad. As one respondent said, it depends on whom you ask. I think it's safe to say that the image of librarians is definitely changing.

However, it's also safe to say that it isn't changing into the clear-cut view of librarianship that we'd like; there's still a lot of simplicity, techno-ignorance, frumpiness, and a tendency toward shushing being displayed. But, it seems better than a decade ago, and we can only keep working toward that future. Educate, assist, inform!

Appendix B

Where's the Librarian? Patrons' Views of Public Perception in the Internet Age

After finding out what we *perceive* to be patrons' perceptions of librarians, I thought it was time to ask the patrons directly. This is a summary of the results of the 2003 "Where's the Librarian?" survey and follow-up talk, which you can see (complete with lovely graphs and fun images) online at the "Where's the Librarian?" website (www.librarian-image.net/wheres_the_librarian.html). (I have to admit to certain preconceived expectations for these survey results based on the librarian survey results, and also on what I see in my own public libraries on a regular basis.)

Survey and Methodology

Over three months in mid-2003, the following libraries graciously allowed me to post a link to my survey on both their main and catalog webpages:

- Tucson-Pima Public Library, Tucson, Arizona (www.library.pima.gov)

- Pierce County Community College, Washington (www.pierce.ctc.edu/library)

- UW-Madison Woodman Astronomical Library, Madison, Wisconsin (astronomy.library.wisc.edu)

- Washburn University's School of Law DocLawWeb, Topeka, Kansas (www.washlaw.edu/doclaw)

- Stratford Library Association, Stratford, Connecticut (www.stratford.lib.ct.us)

- Solano County Libraries, California (www.solanolibrary.com)

- European Southern Observatory Library, Chile (www.eso.org/sci/libraries)

- Tarrant County Law Library, Fort Worth, Texas (www.tarrantcounty.com/eLaw/site)

The survey questions were:

- How old are you?

- How long have you been using the library?

- How often do you use the library?

- Do you use the library's online catalog?

- Do you ask the librarian for help with the online catalog?

- Do you use the library's computers for Internet access (i.e., not library-specific)?

- Do you ask the librarian for help with your Internet use?

- Would you be comfortable talking to:

  - A male/female librarian?

  - A younger/older librarian?

  - A conservatively/casually dressed librarian?

- Do you think a librarian needs a college degree?

- Do you think that anyone who works in a library is a librarian?

I received 782 responses to the survey, although not every respondent answered every question. I need to mention that the results may be skewed; I had intended this to be a patron-only survey, but did not clarify that I would rather librarians not complete it, even though they are patrons, too. I also learned a great deal about how to build a survey for the general public—especially about word choice and selection order. The survey link was also sent around to other lists, college departments, and book groups, so many respondents were not actually sitting at a library computer. (Of course, given the location-independent nature of the web, there's no guarantee that any of the respondents were actually sitting at a library computer.)

Survey Results

How old are you? I was hoping for a nice demographic representation of the general populace, and I got it. Teenagers, 20-somethings, all the way through. This is a nice curve, and I was especially glad to get some young folks in on the survey.

How long have you been using the library? This is where I suspect we start getting the "librarian skew," as three-quarters of the respondents have been using the library for more than 10 years. But the other quarter is what I was expecting, a bit more of a balance across the options, from "I've been using the library forever" to "I just walked into one for the first time yesterday."

How old are you?

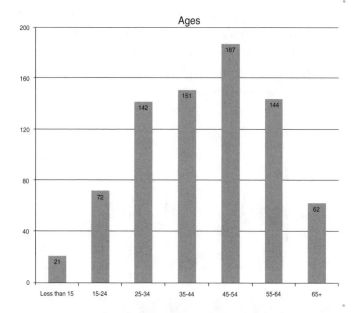

How long have you been using the library?

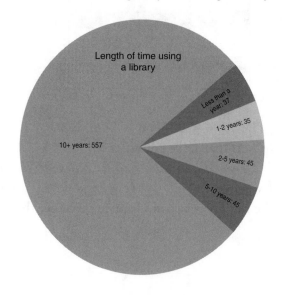

How often do you use the library? I'm amused by the fact that seven people said "never"—I am assuming those people weren't sitting at a library computer while filling out this survey! I like that the majority answer was "several times a month," although of course I'd be happier with several times a week.

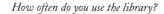

How often do you use the library?

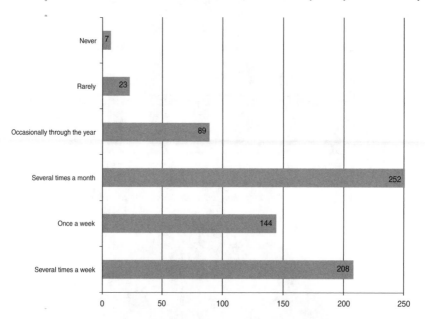

Do you use the library's online catalog? I was very happy to find that folks are using it.

Do you ask the librarian for help with the online catalog? I was sad to find out that respondents weren't using all the resources at hand to help them get the most out of it.

Do you use the library's online catalog?

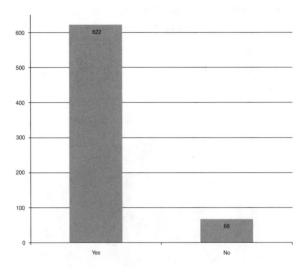

Do you ask the librarian for help with the online catalog?

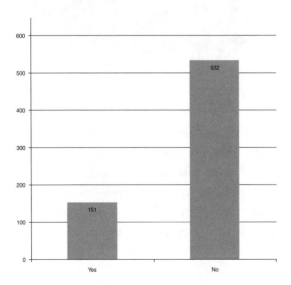

Do you use the library's computers for Internet access (i.e., not library-specific)? Based on my own experience, I expected these numbers to be reversed. Every time I go into my local library every single terminal is full of people surfing the web, checking their email, and just checking things out online.

Do you use the library's computer for Internet access?

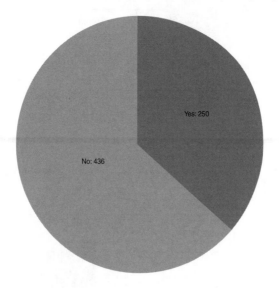

Yes: 250

No: 436

Do you ask the librarian for help with your Internet use? Unfortunately, the majority of respondents answered "no." I hope this trend changes.

Would you be comfortable talking to... It's good to see that, at least in real life, it doesn't seem to matter how the librarian appears, as long as they're approachable.

Do you ask the librarian for help with your Internet use?

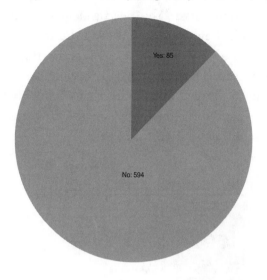

Yes: 85

No: 594

Would you be comfortable talking to ...

	Yes	No
A male librarian	92.7%	7.2%
A female librarian	97.2%	2.8%
An older librarian	93.1%	6.8%
A younger librarian	92.7%	7.3%
A conservatively dressed librarian	89.3%	1.1%
A casually dressed librarian	93.9%	6.1%

Do you think a librarian needs a college degree? Based on comments like "You need a degree to do that?", what I read in newspapers, and even the results of the first survey, I did expect the answers to this question to be reversed. This may partially be due to librarians answering the survey, but I believe this is largely because people are beginning to appreciate the training that goes into becoming a librarian.

Do you think a librarian needs a college degree?

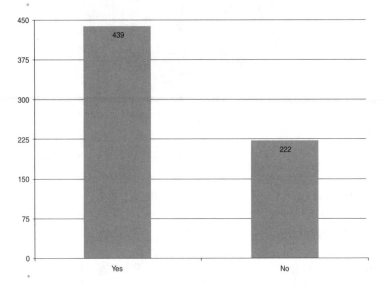

Do you think that anyone who works in a library is a librarian? This is the big question. There may be some "librarian skew" here, too, but not enough to sling the numbers like this. Because of the recent deluge of online articles, webcasts, and newspaper articles about librarians, the public may be starting to see that this is

Do you think that anyone who works in a library is a librarian?

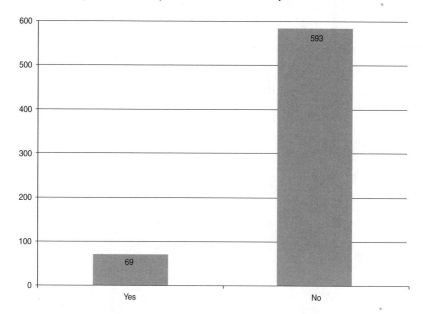

a profession that requires attention, detail, care, and diligence, and it takes extra training to do what we do.

Overall, media representations notwithstanding, things seem to be heading in the right direction. All we can do is what we've been doing: educate, assist, and inform!

References and Other Resources

Introduction

Burns, Grant. *Librarians in Fiction: A Critical Bibliography.* Jefferson, NC: McFarland & Company, Inc., 1998: 1.

Hall, Bill. "The Sadder But Wiser Librarian for Me." *Lewiston (Idaho) Tribune* September 19, 2001.

Kneale, Ruth. Random Musings from the Desert. desertlibrarian.blogspot.com

Kneale, Ruth. You Don't Look Like a Librarian! www.librarian-image.net

Chapter 1

Acerro, Heather, Adrienne Allen, Cheryl Bartel, DarLynn Nemitz, and Dana Vinke. "Image of Libraries in Popular Culture." New York University. besser.tsoa.nyu.edu/impact/f01/Focus/Image/index.htm

Arant, Wendi, and Candace Benefiel. *The Image and Role of the Librarian*. Binghamton, NY: Haworth Press, 2002: 2.

Bowes, Barry. *Between the Stacks*. London: Landesman, 1979: 7.

Brewerton, Antony. "Wear Lipstick, Have a Tattoo, Belly-dance, Then Get Naked: The Making of a Virtual Librarian." *Impact: Journal of the Career Development Group* 2:0 (November–December 1999). tinyurl.com/6lffhk

Cole, Maureen, ed. "Lively Librarians Loose in the Limelight: Libraries in Popular Media." *OLA Quarterly*. Spring 2008. tinyurl.com/6n4g7m

Low, Kathleen. *Casanova Was a Librarian*. Jefferson NC: McFarland Publishing, 2007. www.casanovawasa librarian.com

Miller, William, and Rita Pellen, eds. *The Reference Librarian*. Philadelphia: Haworth Press, Inc. www.haworthpress.com/store/product.asp?sku=J120

Rochkind, Jonathan. "Brain Drain?" Bibliographic Wilderness. February 4, 2008. bibwild.wordpress. com/2008/02/04/brain-drain

Seale, Maura. "Old Maids, Policemen, and Social Rejects: Mass Media Representations and Public Perceptions of Librarians." *Electronic Journal of Academic and Special Librarianship* 9: 1 (Spring 2008). southernlibrarianship.icaap.org/content/v09n01/seale _m01.html

Chapter 2

Abbott, Jeff. *Jordan Poteet* series. New York: Random House, 1994–1996. www.jeffabbott.com

Alexander, William. "In Praise of Librarian Warriors." Powell's Books Review. June 22, 2008. tinyurl.com/3n3fn9

Ambaum, Gene, and Bill Barnes. *Unshelved*. Overdue Media LLC, 2002–present. www.unshelved.com

"Barbara Gordon." Wikipedia. en.wikipedia.org/wiki/Barbara_Gordon

Beinhart, Larry. *The Librarian*. New York: Avalon Publishing Group, 2004. www.thelibrarian.biz

Birdie. "LISNews Interview With Librarian Nancy Pearl." *LIS News* August 9, 2005. lisnews.org/node/15750

Block, Melissa. "Librarians to the Rescue: New Action Figure Salutes Unsung Heroes." *National Public Radio* September 1, 2003. www.npr.org/templates/story/story.php?storyId=1415714

Braun, Lillian Jackson. The *Cat Who …* series. New York: Dutton Books, 1966–2008.

"*Buffy the Vampire Slayer*." Wikipedia. en.wikipedia.org/wiki/Buffy_the_Vampire_Slayer_(TV_series)

Burns, Grant. *Librarians in Fiction*. Jefferson, NC: McFarland Publishing, 1998.

Campbell, Corinne. "Reaching the Promised Land: An Interview with Eugenie Prime." *Information Outlook* January 1997. tinyurl.com/2jh2dt

Carlson, Johanna Draper. "Congratulations to Unshelved." Comics Worth Reading. February 21, 2007. comicsworthreading.com/2007/02/21/congratulations-to-unshelved

DeCandido, GraceAnne. "Rupert Giles and Search Tools for Wisdom in *Buffy the Vampire Slayer*." 2001. www.well.com/user/ladyhawk/Giles.html

Dereske, Jo. *Miss Zukas* mystery series. New York: Avon Books, 1994–2008. www.jodereske.com

Dueben, Alex. "The Modern Library: Barnes talks *Unshelved*." *Comic Book Resource News* October 18, 2007. www.comicbookresources.com/?page=article&id=11737

Ellis, Rhett. *How I Fell in Love with a Librarian and Lived to Tell About It*. Mobile, AL: Sparkling Bay Books, 2003.

Fast, Margaret. "Book Lust and the Digitized Librarian: An Interview with Nancy Pearl." Habits of Waste: A Quarterly Review of Pop Culture. November 2007. www.habitsofwaste.wwu.edu/issues/7/iss7art3a.shtml

Highsmith, Doug. "The Long, Strange Trip of Barbara Gordon: Images of Librarians in Comic Books." *The Image and Role of the Librarian*. Binghamton, NY: Haworth Press, 2002: 81.

"*Jack of Fables*." Wikipedia. en.wikipedia.org/wiki/Jack_of_Fables

Kostova, Elizabeth. *The Historian*. New York: Time Warner Books, 2005. the-historian.net

"*The Librarian* Franchise." Wikipedia.
en.wikipedia.org/wiki/The_Librarian_franchise

"Librarians Oppose Shushing Action Figure." *CNN*
September 8, 2003. www.cnn.com/2003/US/
West/09/08/offbeat.librarian.ap/index.html

"Nancy Pearl." Wikipedia.
en.wikipedia.org/wiki/Nancy_Pearl

Niffenegger, Audrey. *The Time Traveler's Wife*. Orlando,
FL: Harcourt Inc., 2003.

"Outcry over Librarian Doll." *Sidney Morning Herald*
September 6, 2003. www.smh.com.au/
articles/2003/09/06/1062549053713.html

"*Party Girl*." Internet Movie Database.
us.imdb.com/title/tt0114095

Peck, Richard. *Here Lies the Librarian*. New York:
Penguin Books, 2006.

Peters, Elizabeth. *Jacqueline Kirby* series. New York:
Mysterious Press, 1972–1989.
www.mpmbooks.com/jkirby/index.html

Plourde, Denise. Library Cartoons: An Annotated
Bibliography. pw1.netcom.com/~dplourde/
cartoons/index.html

Pratchett, Terry. *Discworld* series. New York:
HarperCollins, 1983–2008. www.terrypratchett
books.com

"*Read or Die*." Wikipedia,
en.wikipedia.org/wiki/Read_or_Die

Samson, Ian. *Mobile Library Mysteries*. New York:
HarperCollins, 2006–2008. www.iansansom.net

"*The Sandman* (Vertigo)." Wikipedia. en.wikipedia.org/wiki/Sandman_(Vertigo)

Seale, Maura. "Old Maids, Policemen, and Social Rejects: Mass Media Representations and Public Perceptions of Librarians." *Electronic Journal of Academic and Special Librarianship* 9:1 (Spring 2008). southernlibrarianship.icaap.org/content/v09n01/seale_m01.html

Sisario, Ben. "Out of the Comfort Zone, Into the Wild Rock Yonder." *New York Times* June 15, 2008. tinyurl.com/65pltx

"SNMNMNM Will Crawl Inside Your Head." Rock Sellout Blog. August 11, 2007. rocksellout.com/2007/08/11/snmnmnm-will-crawl-inside-your-head

Tobias, Jenny. "AdLib: The Advertised Librarian; The Image Is the Message." *Information Outlook* February 2003. tinyurl.com/5tc2fn

Turner, James. "Ordo Bibliotheca." www.jtillustration.com/rex/ordo_bibliotheca.html

Chapter 3

Credaro, Amanda. *Biblia's Guide to Warrior Librarianship.* Portsmouth, NH: Libraries Unlimited, 2003.

Levine, Jenny. "Gaming in Libraries." *ALA TechSource* 44: 3 (April 2008). www.techsource.ala.org/ltr/gaming-and-libraries-intersection-of-services.html

Library Student Journal. www.librarystudentjournal.org

Chapter 4

Abels, Eileen, Rebecca Jones, John Latham, Dee Magnoni, and Joanne Gard Marshall. "Competencies for Information Professionals." Special Libraries Association. June 2003. www.sla.org/content/learn/comp2003/index.cfm

Akerman, Richard. "The Public Library Is for: the Public." Science Library Pad. July 22, 2008. tinyurl.com/5afnrq

Bell, Steven, et al. "Changing Roles of Academic and Research Libraries." Association of College and Research Libraries. April 18, 2007. www.ala.org/ala/mgrps/divs/acrl/issues/future/changingroles.cfm

Brewerton, Antony. "Wear Lipstick, Have a Tattoo, Belly-dance, Then Get Naked: The Making of a Virtual Librarian." *Impact: Journal of the Career Development Group* 2:0 November–December 1999. tinyurl.com/6lffhk

Curry, Anne. "Public Space and Libraries." University of British Columbia. tinyurl.com/5clpgv

"Cybrary City." Wikipedia. www.libsuccess.org/index.php?title=Cybrary_City

"Digital divide." Wikipedia. en.wikipedia.org/wiki/Digital_divide

Engard, Nicole, and Leslie Reynolds. "Key Takeaways from the Keynote Speakers." *bITe* 25:3 (Summer 2008). units.sla.org/division/dite/bite/2008/bITe Summer2008.pdf

Farkas, Meredith. "Skills for the 21st Century Librarian." Information Wants to Be Free. July 17, 2006. tinyurl.com/pp6jq

Fogle, D. Lynn, et al. *The Changing Role of Law Firm Librarianship.* Boston: Aspatore Books, 2008.

Fried, Benjamin, and Jay Walljasper. "Project for Public Spaces April 2007 Newsletter." April 2007. www.pps.org/info/newsletter/april2007

Ghikas, Mary, et al. "Statement of Core Competencies." American Library Association. June 2008. wikis.ala.org/professionaltips/index.php/competencies

Guevara, Sophie. "Digital Focus: Interview with Michael Stephens." *bITe* 25:3 (Summer 2008). units.sla.org/division/dite/bite/2008/bITeSummer 2008.pdf

Horrigan, John. "Broadband: What's All the Fuss About?" Pew Internet & American Life Project, Reports on Technology and Media Use. October 8, 2007. www.pewinternet.org/PPF/r/224/report_ display.asp

Kim, Eugene. "The Intellectual Foundation of Information Organization." *WebTechniques.* New Architect. December 2001. webtechniques.com/ archives/2001/12/book

Long, Sarah. "Technology Is Changing Role of
    Librarian into That of a Teacher." Our Libraries
    column. *Chicago Daily Herald* November 28, 2005.
    www.librarybeat.org/read/show/233

Ramos, Mila. "The Role of Librarians in the 21st
    Century." Presentation at the 35th ALAP
    Anniversary Forum, June 8, 2007. tinyurl.com/5ht7co

"SLA 2008 Conference Hosts 5,000-Plus." *Information
    Outlook* 12:7 (July 2008).

WEBSITES

Websites are listed in the order that they appear. Find this list of links at the accompanying webpage (www. librarian-image.net/book).

Chapter 1

Marathon County Public Library,
www.lisnews.org/node/29261

Real Job Titles for Librarians and Information Science Professionals (Michelle Mach),
www.michellemach.com/jobtitles/realjobs.html

U.S. Bureau of Labor Statistics, www.bls.gov

U.S. Bureau of Labor Statistics: Librarian (2000),
stats.bls.gov/oes/2000/oes254021.htm

U.S. Bureau of Labor Statistics: Database Administrator (2000), stats.bls.gov/oes/2000/oes151061.htm

U.S. Bureau of Labor Statistics: Librarian (2007),
www.bls.gov/oes/current/oes254021.htm

U.S. Bureau of Labor Statistics: Database Administrator (2007), www.bls.gov/oes/current/oes151061.htm

U.S. Bureau of Labor Statistics: Computer Science and Database Administrators (2008–2009), www.bls.gov/oco/ocos042.htm

Monster.com, www.monster.com

Monster.com Salary Center: Librarian, tinyurl.com/6bcylr

Monster.com Salary Center: Database Administrator, tinyurl.com/6j7x77

Monster.com Salary Center: Webmaster, tinyurl.com/6e9n6k

Brain Drain (Bibliographic Wilderness), bibwild. wordpress.com/2008/02/04/brain-drain

New Breed Librarian, scholarsbank.uoregon.edu/dspace/handle/1794/1071

Wear Lipstick, Have a Tattoo, Belly-dance, Then Get Naked: The Making of a Virtual Librarian (*Impact: Journal of the Career Development Group*), tinyurl.com/6lffhk

Image of Libraries in Popular Culture, besser.tsoa.nyu.edu/impact/f01/Focus/Image/index.htm

"SSSSHHHHHH!!!!!, stereotypicallibrarian.blogspot.com

Library Journal's NextGen column, www.libraryjournal.com (search for "NextGen")

Libraries, Archives, Museums, and Popular Culture
Area (Popular Culture Association),
www.pcaaca.org/areas/libraries.php

Librarian Sexuality sites (Warning: adult content),
www.libraryunderground.org/sexuality.htm

No, I Don't Look Like a Librarian!,
www.facebook.com/group.php?gid=2251972614

Yes, I Do Look Like a Librarian!,
www.facebook.com/group.php?gid=2272645001

Chapter 2

Librarians in Comic Books, www.ibiblio.org/libraries
faq/combks/combks.htm

Librarians in Comic Strips, www.ibiblio.org/libraries
faq/comstrp/comstrp.htm

Unshelved, www.unshelved.com

Rex Libris, www.jtillustration.com/rex

Shelf Check, shelfcheck.blogspot.com

Tom the Dancing Bug, www.tomthedancingbug.com

Frazz, www.comics.com/comics/frazz

Speed Bump, www.speedbump.com

Turn the Page, librarycartoons.blogspot.com

Questionable Content, www.questionablecontent.net

Librarians in the Movies: An Annotated Filmography,
emp.byui.edu/RAISHM/films/introduction.html

The Film Librarian, www.filmlibrarian.info

The Mummy movies, www.themummy.com

The Hollywood Librarian, www.hollywoodlibrarian.com

BlöödHag, www.bloodhag.com

"Librarian" by Haunted Love,
   www.youtube.com/watch?v=Ne_WXP7lUWM

A New Song for the Modern Librarian (addwillknow),
   addywillknow.pbwiki.com

MySpace: SNMNMNM, www.myspace.com/
   snmnmnm

"Librarian" by My Morning Jacket, tinyurl.com/3t46ny

"Every Time we Touch" by Cascada,
   www.youtube.com/watch?v=ZK0GmiSMNGI

Between the Lions, pbskids.org/lions

Australian Broadcasting Company's "The Librarians."
   www.abc.net.au/tv/librarians/

The Librarians,
   www.australiantelevision.net/librarians/episodes.html

Honda Accord ad, www.librarian-
   image.net/img02/honda_librariancar.jpg

Bacardi ad, www.librarian-image.net/img02/bacardi.jpg

Hewlitt-Packard ad, tinyurl.com/6dvtqd

DHL ad, www.youtube.com/watch?v=tz8L0oLIyak

Go, Socks! (Laughing Librarian), www.laughing
   librarian.com/2005_10_01_archive.html

Sony ad and discussion,
   www.flickr.com/photos/albaum/1356519239

Sony's Reader: Sexier than a Librarian?
news.sel.sony.com/electronicsblog/?p=23

Archie McPhee, www.mcphee.com

Librarian Action Figure, www.mcphee.com/laf

LISNews Interview with Librarian Nancy Pearl,
lisnews.org/node/15750

Book Lust and the Digitized Librarian: An Interview
with Nancy Pearl,
www.habitsofwaste.wwu.edu/issues/7/iss7art3a.shtml

Questionable Content merchandise, www.questionable
content.net/merch.php

Rex Libris merchandise, www.slgcomic.com/James-
Turner_c_56-1.html

CafePress, www.cafepress.com

The Renaissance Library Collection, www.renaissance
library.com

UHF "Conan the Librarian" video, tinyurl.com/2pwvwt

William Mitchell College of Law's "Conan the
Librarian" adventures, tinyurl.com/jq7r

Chapter 3

Special Libraries Association, www.sla.org

Stephen's Lighthouse, stephenslighthouse.sirsidynix.com

American Library Association, www.ala.org

Researching @ Eller Blog,
blog.ltc.arizona.edu/researchingateller

- SlideShare, slideshare.net
- PBwiki, washalr.pbwiki.com
- WashLaw, www.washlaw.edu
- Fifth Circuit Court of Appeals Law Library, www.lb5.uscourts.gov
- Hurst Associates Ltd., www.hurstassociates.com
- Pikes Peak Library District, library.ppld.org
- Pikes Peak Library District Teen Zone Blog, library.ppld.org/blogs/teen
- Pikes Peak Library District Teen Zone Message Board, www.websitetoolbox.com/tool/mb/teenzone
- Pikes Peak Library District Teen Zone MySpace page, myspace.com/pikespeaklibraryteens
- Pikes Peak Library District Teen Zone Booktalks, ppldbooktalks.podbean.com
- University of Notre Dame Libraries, www.library.nd.edu
- ALA TechSource Gaming, Learning, and Libraries Symposium, gaming.techsource.ala.org
- National Gaming in Libraries Day, www.ilovelibraries.org/gaming
- The Shifted Librarian, www.theshiftedlibrarian.com
- Yale University Science Libraries, www.library.yale.edu/science/socialnetworking.html
- Johnson County Library, www.jocolibrary.org
- JoCoKids, www.jocokids.org
- JoCoTeenScene, www.jocoteenscene.org

OPAL (Online Programming for All Libraries),
www.opal-online.org

University of Hawaii Institute for Astronomy Library,
www.ifa.hawaii.edu/library

Uniform Data System for Medical Rehabilitation,
www.udsmr.org

The Bellydancing Librarian,
www.sonic.net/~erisw/bdlib.html

Tribe.net: Bellydancing Librarians, tribes.tribe.net/
bellydancinglibrarians

Butt Kicking Librarians, hokkien.uuft.org/librarian.html

Facebook, www.facebook.com

No, I don't look like a librarian!,
www.facebook.com/group.php?gid=2251972614

Yes, I do look like a librarian,
www.facebook.com/group.php?gid=2272645001

Do I look like a librarian?, www.facebook.com/group.
php?gid=2262934453

I'm a librarian, but I'm not old, I don't own many cats,
and work nights,
www.facebook.com/group.php?gid=2263762244

Librarians who Twitter,
www.facebook.com/group.php?gid=5825485883

Tattooed Librarians,
www.facebook.com/group.php?gid=2431775521

Librarians with tudes!,
www.facebook.com/group.php?gid=2228255511

Sexy librarians,
www.facebook.com/group.php?&gid=2204977608

Second Life librarians,
www.facebook.com/group.php?&gid=2395106896

WoW (World of Warcraft) librarians,
www.facebook.com/group.php?&gid=5200354786

The Laughing Librarian, www.laughinglibrarian.com

Librarian Avengers, librarianavengers.org

Cory Doctorow at ALA, tinyurl.com/5qmtx4

Library Society of the World, librarysociety.pbwiki.com
or thelsw.org

Library Underground, www.libraryunderground.org

Lipstick Librarian, www.lipsticklibrarian.com

Archie McPhee's Illustrated Librarian Temporary
Tattoos, www.mcphee.com/items/11696.html

Modified Librarians, www.bmeworld.com/gailcat

Radical Reference Librarians, www.radicalreference.info

The Warrior Librarian, www.warriorlibrarian.com

Chapter 4

Encyclopedia Galactica: Librarian,
www.orionsarm.com/eg/l/Li-Ln.html#librarian

Seth Godin, www.sethgodin.com

Create Change, www.createchange.org

Gartner Research Group, www.gartner.com

Second Life, secondlife.com

Alliance Library System,
www.alliancelibrarysystem.com

Info Island, infoisland.org

Pew Internet & American Life Project, www.pew
internet.org

Pew Internet & American Life Project: Demographics of
Internet Users, www.pewinternet.org/trends/User_
Demo_10%2020%2008.htm

Pew Internet & American Life Project: Broadband
2008, www.pewinternet.org/PPF/r/257/report_
display.asp

Public Spaces and Libraries, tinyurl.com/5clpgv

The Public Library Is for: the Public (Science Library
Pad), tinyurl.com/5afnrq

Project for Public Spaces April 2007 Newsletter,
www.pps.org/info/newsletter/april2007

Libraries for the Future, www.lff.org

East Lansing Public Library Recommendations,
www.elpl.org/patronreviews.htm

Butler University Libraries' Reference Wiki, www.seed
wiki.com/wiki/butler_wikiref

Hennepin County Library BookSpace,
www.hclib.org/pub/bookspace

BiblioCommons, bibliocommons.com

Oakville Public Library, www.opl.on.ca

Darien Library, www.darienlibrary.org

- Ann Arbor District Library catalog, www.aadl.org/catalog
- SOPAC 2.0: What to Expect (blyberg.net), www.blyberg.net/2008/08/16/sopac-20-what-to-expect
- Tame the Web, www.tametheweb.com
- Women in Science and Education program at the University of Arizona, ws.web.arizona.edu/wise
- The Blended Librarian, www.blendedlibrarian.org

About the Author

Ruth Kneale is the Systems Librarian
for the Advanced Technology Solar
Telescope in Tucson, Arizona. Prior to
that, she was the Librarian and
Webmaster for the Gemini Observatory
in Hilo, Hawaii, and the Gemini 8m
Telescopes Project (what observatories
are before they grow up) in Tucson.
Basically, she's a librarian in geek
clothing, whose first program was created using BASIC on a TRS-80 with a
tape drive. Ruth holds a master's
degree in Information Resources and

Library Science from the University of Arizona and a
Bachelor of Science in Astronomy and Physics. An Air
Force brat, she grew up all over the world before settling
in the desert and becoming a cold-weather wimp.

Ruth has written on computer topics for *Information
Outlook* and *Computers in Libraries*, and publishes a regular column about librarians in *Marketing Library Services*

called "Spectacles: How Pop Culture Views Librarians." Even though she lives in Arizona, she's also written twice for the Oregon Library Association about pop culture and librarians. She has presented several times at the Special Libraries Association annual meetings and at Internet Librarian. She started the website You Don't Look Like a Librarian! (www.librarian-image.net) in 2002, and a companion blog called Random Musings from the Desert (desertlibrarian.blogspot.com) in 2006.

Ruth's favorite color is purple, her favorite airplane is the A-10 Warthog (properly called the Thunderbolt II), and she has a secret collection of 1980s Euro-pop in her iPod.

INDEX